AF413266

THE REASON WHY 2

By

Johnny Collins

ACKNOWLEDGEMENT

First and foremost, I want to say R.I.P. to the falling soldiers, but I want to take the time out to say, that if you lost a love one to the hands of racism whether it be by the police, or somebody underneath a sheet, or bare faced. One is no different than the next, but my respect to you and yours as I too know what it's like to lose someone close by a reckless off duty police officer. I love you Montana, its "SA" forever, always South-side. Shout out to my mother Shirley Fallings who grind me up constantly cause she wants me to use my talents in the studio, I will for you mommy. But I wrote this novel, not for people to remember why they were angry, and I didn't write it to encourage you to bust your gun every time that you see the police.

Understand, to me 5-0 is 5.0 to me, but also, I respect the human species, that's God's work. I wrote this for not just white people, or black people, but for all races to have a visual emotional attachment, to what is real life for the Afrikan inside America since the beginning of us landing here. Believe me, I wish those of us that may have been kidnapped would have either escaped, or died in the act of escape, and we wouldn't be having this conversation, and a lot of Africans would still be alive. In my time of living over forty years, I've had many conversations with a lot of white people who didn't know their own history, or the history between the Americans and Africans. Hearing the ignorant speak use to upset me, is when I realized that you could learn a lot from a dummy. I had the opportunity to bring light where there was darkness, but in the course of teaching, I too was learning from these individuals. But I used to always hear white people or house niggers on TV, like CNN, or HLN, C-Span, etc..., but these people always spoke on these topics when asked their input or opinions on what they thought when a black person was falsely placed in prison, or killed by police, and it always came off as if it was that person's fault. Then I really lost it when the president spoke of putting an end to civil law suits for false imprisonment knowing the African American race is the number one race to end up in prison for false allegations, or mistaken identity, etc..., but it showed me how far we've came as a people in America, which was not very far. With people like this in power from the courtroom to the Bill room playing dictator. We will always be oppressed. I don't need my family waking up every morning giving up before they had a chance to wash their face and brush their teeth. Those tactics used by the European race is a strategy used to keep niggers in their place, as was taught by generations before those who control the power now. Living life like this for so many years stunts the growth of your reception capacity causing you to compartmentalize your brain. Causing you to use a very small percentage of your brain. This has caused most of us to be trapped up in our own minds running the hamster wheel going nowhere. If you teach a baby to kill as the baby starts to grow, it becomes normal to the child, second nature. This is what we are teaching our babies by teaching them nothing about who they really are. I've been asking questions since I could speak, and everyone would always run out of answers, so I took it upon myself to research where it is I came from and who I was supposed to be is KING!

Your child should never feel uncomfortable in their skin because they feel as if white people are rich and privileged. I know a lot of you to have to work long hours, but the time that you are home, remove them from those games and phones. Always make sure they stay woke or they become a product of the prison that's being forced on them through advertisement. Not to get away from my point, this was to show how leadership and sacrifice are important elements through determination. These are sometimes important elements through determination. These are sometimes the things that have to happen in life for people to wake up and come together. It shouldn't have to be this way, but history has never changed its ingredients, it is us who has to change ours in order for the earth to change its course. Mankind is just about nearly wiped out every few thousand years due to the human species disorder in the ways in which we live. I shouldn't have to ask for anything, but I was raised with manner so I will. Imagine this book a real situation that took place, we know why it took place. But dissect this book and find ways or different things that you could have done or do to prevent a future situation, or to better yourself or another individual. We need to better prepare ourselves for situations that can be this, or similar to it with the way we treat each other. Its past due those times where you can treat people with such a great deal of disrespect and expect no repercussion is absurd. Respect it and live to love your neighbor.

Table of Contents

CHAPTER 1

Quincey looked at Jeff, "Your Honor, if you will". Jeff went and put on a robe he brought from home, and had a mallet for his gravel coated in rubber, set up a chair and put a small table in front of the chair, and sat down. "Now, this is the Honorable Jeff, since you cops like to have these rigged trials, knowing it takes the power away from the jurors. See our judge is a fair or impartial one who will do as he swore, and that is to uphold the law, something you government officials know nothing about. Anyway, I'll be your local prosecutor who happens to work for the people. You will not have thirty minutes to prepare, there will be no plea agreements, use your time wisely gentlemen". Quincey went and put on a suit jacket and returned.

Benjamin started to sweat and blurted out, "Wait a minute, what the hell is this you tryna' pull off? You can't do this, this isn't how the court works". "I can see you never been black before. You get to experience everything the brother man goes through. See how you already been kidnapped, living conditions aren't good, the guards hadn't been feeding you three meals a day, you ain't got no clean sheets nor uniforms. Hell, you've been getting your ass whooped last time I checked, those are all the things ya'll do to us. Benjamin was trying to buy his self some time so he said, "Your Honor, May I approach the bench?"

Jeff looked at Quincey who broke out laughing, "Ahem", he cleared his throat, "I apologize for my outburst your Honor, look, just imagine that you are standing in front of the bench, speak as long as you want, but remember your time is winding down and you don't have that much time left to prepare and present your case". "May I remind you Mr. Taggart, you have a lot of work to do to persuade the court". Jeff banged his gravel and said, "Alright you have two minutes", he looked at his watch and said, "Let's proceed". "Who would like to go first?" "Why am I here, I don't even...". "Got a volunteer in the center right here, could you state your name for the record please?" "This is absurd..." Quincey stormed over him and said, "You've been warned", then he looked over at Jeff and said, "Sorry your Honor, he was being unreasonable". "I will allow it", Jeff banged his gravel again and said, "Listen gentlemen, court is in session, let the commonwealth proceed".

"Ladies and gentlemen, I present to you a case where an officer of the law failed to do his job. A young man was murdered in cold blood, because a racist and a drunk cop felt he shouldn't be alive!" Quincey raised his tone and pointed at Benjamin, "He had the power to do so based on the white privilege theory". White privilege means, Europeans, white Anglo Saxon, fake Jews, English, all the same. These people who believe that they are better than all other races, especially blacks! Because of this slave epidemic that never left my people, your people, created this false belief that you were superior to all of God's creations, created the myth that you were royal bloodline of the deities and God's chosen people. And not to be funny, but out of all the places on God's green earth, you would want us to believe that you would pick the hottest places on the planet to live, but also post pictures of a white Christ in all of your churches on this cross that didn't even exist in his time. When they say, "take up your burden", they were talking about one slab of wood that only existed in certain parts of the world. "So what was, or whose ideal was it to alter the books in the bible, adding European names, but you don't alter the description of Christ? Now, I don't know any white men with burnt feet unless he has a prosthetic one. God put you in a position to punish my people, and you abused it, and today, your time is up". Quincey looked around and said, "I will prove to you the allegations of first degree murder, hate crimes, etc..." "Mr. DeJesus, do you have an open argument?" "I didn't do any of those things, he did. I..." "Alright, that is enough. Do the commonwealth wish to go ahead with any questions?" "I do your Honor". "You may proceed".

"Mr. DeJesus, you are a conspirator in the alleged accusations, when your partner got out of that car harassing those children on their way to school. Why didn't you interfere?" "What do you mean, I did". "How so?" "I told him to get back in the car. I could tell he'd been drinking". "And you still got in the car with him while driving under the influence? Isn't that against the law...and you failed to take his keys and report the incident?" "Well...I...I..." "Right, you neglected your duty as a government official. So now, after you helped him get to the point of murder, "Quincey's tone went up again, "you stood there while your partner pulled that trigger...multiple times...and you was like a bitch trapped in headlights. You didn't call for help, and you didn't try to help. Your cod tells you to lie, and lie fluently...being one of the good ol' boy". He stormed back over and slapped Hector DeJesus extremely hard that he could taste blood in his mouth. "Let that part be stricken from the record your Honor." Jeff asked if Quincey was done proceeding before he decided to give Hector the floor. "The commonwealth rest your Honor." "Mr. DeJesus, I am going to give you a chance to defend yourself, but first I must warm you that you are under oath. You may proceed". "What am I to say?" "That is up to you". Benjamin was thinking to himself, "No one was even sworn in", but he was trying to think of a way to get out of his situation, that he even thought about playing sleep. Hector had already decided that he was going to die anyway, so he just figured that honesty was the best way to go, so when he's dead they would all know the truth. "I had no knowledge that he would kill that kid, I was only in the car with him because nobody wanted to ride with me because I was Mexican. I was just trying to fit in and get ahead..." "And how did that work out?" Quincey asked cutting him off. "It didn't, I nearly lost my family because I decided to come clean and tell the truth about what happened. I can't apologize for somebody else's actions, at the end of the day I have to be held accountable for my own. Nothing ever changes if it stays the same, right". Hector said it more to himself than to the others. "I have to live with this guilt for the rest of my life, thinking that I could be one of them". Hector just laid there pondering for a while without saying anything else. "Well I take it that the defense rest".

"Hey", Benjamin said, "Do you think you can cut me loose, it'll be hard for me to express and present any case wrapped up like this. I mean..." "Look, this isn't TV Mr. Taggart. There will not be a second situation where you come up with a last minute ideal with the belief that once your cut loose, you could over power somebody and kill us all, right. Not today", Quincey didn't even care to hear Benjamin's defense. "Are you presenting your case or not Mr. Taggart?" "I'm going to die anyway, or spend the rest of my life incarcerated. Your daddy would have been very disappointed in you boy, and you", he said looking at Quincey, "You come from the shit scraped off the bottom of God's shoe boy! I'll fucking gut you boy if I wasn't like this here...coward!" He tried to spit on Quincey missing him by nearly an inch and a half, in a swift motion, Quincey grabbed the mallet they used as a substitute for a gravel. Benjamin eyes widened when he saw Quincey cock back and swing it like a polo mallet, he knew the pain would be severe. The impact from the strike shattered Benjamin's jaw bone knocking him unconscious. "His time is definitely coming...real soon". He walked away clutching the handle of the mallet, saying, "Real soon". He grabbed the duct tape from out the tool box and taped their mouth up again and left to get home to deal with his mother if she became suspicious.

When he arrived at home he could smell the hot breakfast aroma escaping the window, he knew they would already be awake for Saturday morning's GI. He didn't bother coming through the window in which the way he left out, no sooner than he walked in the door, he was greeted by his siblings arguing about who could sing or not. "Neither one of ya'll can sing", he said teasing them while making his way in the kitchen. "Boy where you been, and where is you coming from?" "I've been dreaming dreams I wish to never see, and they been keeping me up", he lied, "so I decided to go run and train". "Well I told you a whole lot of crazy stuff has been going on out there, it's too much to take in and I do not need to lose you to some nonsense". "Ya not gonna..." "Boy you don't know what could happen, just like God give, he take as well. Now go on and wash up and come on and eat, and don't think you getting out of cleaning up". "I know mom", he picked his gym bag up, turned back to say something but changed his mind.

After eating breakfast, and helping the family clean the house, Quincey went to clean his room. He turned on his TV and stopped on a news channel, something he hadn't watched in a while, and saw the federal government rounding up some people that were all said to have been on a ten man indictment that was recently unseated. He laughed to himself when seeing the face of Benjamin Taggart posted on the screen, not only listed on the ten man incident, but another one for a slew of hate crimes, including the murder of Trevon with open investigations on two others. Quincey was in deep thought when he couldn't help but hear the clip of business Mogul Teddy McNaire attempt to take his own life. But then started to wonder why when things weren't going well for the white folks who had lived such a good life whether they cheated for it or earned it honestly, why was suicide their first option? The news reporter had mentioned trying to locate Benjamin's whereabouts.

CHAPTER 2

Stacy had been trying to get a hold of Hector to see if he was willing to do an interview for CBS, and patriot one, but first and foremost, to check up on him to see how he was actually doing. Assuming that he might happen to be super busy, she figured that she would call back later, so she did, and still didn't get an answer. She jumped in her car thinking that it might be nothing, and head on over to his house. When she arrived, she saw his car parked on the side of the street where he normally parks. Stacy did a quick observation of her surroundings then got out her car and knocked on the Hectors' door. After no response from around the back, she tried the front again, this time turning the knob. "Hello, Hector. Are you in here?" Stacy thought about all of the drama she had been through in the last few days, and wasn't about to take a chance, so she reached in her coat pocket and brandished her small, 380 semiautomatic hand gun, tip toeing through the house. She didn't see anything out of the ordinary or unusual, so she pulled out her cell phone and called detective Atkins, then called federal Agent Timmothy Cyrus explaining her beliefs. Detective Atkins was the first to arrive at Hector's place. Stacy did not feel comfortable waiting in her car for either of them to arrive because of the time she had to give Hector a ride to the hospital, so she decided to sit on the hood of her car instead, in case something should happen unexpectedly. No sooner than Detective Atkins spoke, did Agent Cyrus pull up and park. "I got here as soon as I could, now what are we thinking might have happened?"

Detective Atkins leaned against Stacy's car waiting to see where the conversation would lead them before he chimed in with his own opinions. "Well he said he was going back to the one place they would least expect him to be, and that is here. But I've been calling him all morning with no answer, so I decided to come back to make sure he was alright, only to find his door unlocked, and an empty house. Now you can call it what you want, but I know he's not going to just leave his house unsecured after all that has happened, and the fact that he just installed a brand new security alarm system". "How do you know he just installed that Ms. Fallings?" "I know he installed it because I've been in the house the day he was almost killed, or kidnapped". "I see...it makes all the sense in the world, but it does disturbs me because we are looking for Benjamin Taggart to bring this list of charges listed from murder and hate crimes, under two different indictments, and when we came to serve him, he was nowhere to be found...and now this". Detective Atkins finally spoke up and said, "Nah, I doubt it. I heard the list of crimes that he's wanted for, and I really don't, or can't believe that a man, even not as quite bright as him, would take the time out, to go look for this one man who also may have been watched for his own safety, but that he would take this knowing that he could be caught in the attempt seems a bit outlandish". "Well", Agent Cyrus paused, "We do have a show for that...the worlds dumbest criminals". They all laughed for a brief moment and became serious all at the same time trying to understand what could have happened. "Well listen, let us try and work the wheel from our end, detective, and Stacy, if you find something out let us know immediately, but please, do not risk your safety to find him on your own".

Quincey made his way back over to check on Benjamin and Hector, feeling as if today was Hectors' lucky day. He was going to allow Hector a chance, or for a better word, an opportunity at redemption. When he arrived to the house, he said to himself, "Yea, that's what I'm going to do, that'll kill two birds with one stone". When he got downstairs in the basement, it appeared to be too quiet, so he yelled, "Wake up gentlemen! Today is one person's lucky day. One". He untapped Benjamin's mouth propping him up, he then went over to Hector whose right arm was also untapped along with his mouth. He then said to Hector, "You got one bullet in the chamber of this here Glock 40. If you put that one bullet, right between his eyes, you get to walk out of here a free man. You have my word", Quincey assured him placing the gun in Hector's hand. He stood behind Hector a few days ago. Hector's hand begun to tremble as he thought the things he could possibly do with the power he possessed. As much as he wanted to pull that beautiful trigger and possibly end all of this that was started by someone who was really unhappy with himself which caused him to actually hate others, it had to be the reason why he done the things he had done throughout his entire life. He didn't deserve to live, but it wasn't his call to say as to who should live or die. He placed the gun on the concrete with tears in his eyes and said, "I can't do it". "No doubt". *BOOM!* Quincey stepped over Hector's body firing another round into his face, and said, "I see he's made his decision, you've been spared again my friend", He looked over at

Benjamin who no longer had that tough guy wall he had built. "Real soon my friend...real soon." Quincey cleaned up his own mess, wrapped Hectors' corpse upon the tarp that he was already sitting next to, taped it up and checked for blood spatter. He then walked over to Benjamin and punched him just because, and said, "you will always remember me, even in death, I promise you".

All Benjamin could do was roll over from the impact of the punch and lay there. He was already weak and famished being as though as he not eaten or drunk anything since he'd been down there. He'd been using the bathroom on himself and all he needed was that one speck of light for a small piece of hope that may never come. Quincey went from humming to his self to talking to his self. "We went from Kings and Queens to being peons in the fields to labor for a race that dare not respect it, respect us as a people, a nation", he expressed poking himself in the chest. It was hard for Quincey to accept the fact that after such deep research of the Afrikan, "How did we come to a time where we allow a race whom we gave birth to, taught civilization to, to kidnap, rob, rape, and slaughter us? But then for a people who knew nothing about fighting, soon as we help, or basically win their independence, treat you even worse than before". Quincey felt that the time was nearing for everything to come to an end, so in between time he was getting his affairs in order. First, he went on-line and auctioned off all of his sports cards for a nice lump sum and he had the checks sent out in his mother's name. He wrote out a will, not for the money to be divided, but instructions for the family to remain strong, and then he gave the reason why as to his actions. He put something to the side for Jeff for when the time should arrive. He decided to send a text to Jeff. "What's up my boy? I need to holla at you in the private". "Soon as I get done eating, my parents got company so you know that they care about family image to the outside world, soon as the company leaves, they'll never know that I'm gone". It was about 6:30 p.m. when Jeff face timed Quincey to inform him that he was bending the corner near the Boys and Girls Club. Jeff learned a lot from Quincey since they had became friends, so it weighed on him knowing that he wanted to meet out of the blue was something that puzzled him.

When they met up, he gave Jeff the normal pound, but went a step further and embraced him. "Man, what was that all about?" "Nothing much, just, you know, you have been there for me through it all. You showed me a loyalty that don't really exist anymore. You risked your life for me, you made a sacrifice not many is willing to make, not even for their own family, feel me?" "I hear you Quincey, but the feeling is mutual, you would have done the same for me. It's not even to be questioned". "I know but I wanted to talk to you about...well you know...it's almost time to end this. But I want you to know that I appreciate you as a best friend, and a person. It's kinda funny when you think back all of those years and the teacher used to ask you what you wanted to be when you grow up...hmm. And to think we knew a lot, nah, my dad had me listen to one of his favorite artist, and you could actually visualize the words he chose to formulate on pad. Hmm, I understand what he meant now. I once valued my life before all of this happened. I actually loved being a kid until I had to grow up overnight, and then I understood the values of being an adult. Every decision is based on everybody's well-being and not just your own. Knowing when to be selfish. I got something that I want you to have, but you will get it soon as everything is over, may not be much, but it's to show my appreciation". "You don't have..." "Yeah, but I needed to. Oh, by the way, I'm a need your help getting that Hector guy out the basement". "What happened?" "I gave him a chance to end it sooner than later, and he turned down the best opportunity...so I had to clean up". "What about the other one?" "He'll be the most famous cop of them all". "And how are you going..." "Jeff, just chill out, you ask too many questions, just trust me on that". When they finished moving Hector's body from the basement to the incinerator, Quincey then decided that he wanted to go and visit Trevon's grave site for the last time to try and find some peace. When Quincey approached the gravesite, he didn't come prepared with a speech or anything of that nature, he just spoke what he felt. "Hmm...my mom always said God has a plan, and I guess the two of us was that plan. You and me homie". He stopped pacing, looked at the sky, then back at the gravesite, "What I mean is...somebody had to die, and somebody had to live...in order for the plan to be carried out. Look at the bigger picture bruh, we was on our way to college, did everything right...and then it was all gone". He snapped his fingers, "See, a small mind ain't open for reception and couldn't comprehend it. You died believing to stand on your own two. Your death was that spark that started the fire that will change history forever". He tapped his chest twice near his heart and said, "Until I join you".

It was already pitch black outside so Quincey said, "Stop at the gas station, I wanna get something, and then shoot to the spot". When he got in the store, he went to the shelf that sold dog food and bought two cans and a gallon of water, then headed back to the van. When they got to the house, Quincey found an old can-opener in the silverware drawer right next to the kitchen sink and opened up a can of dog food, when Jeff asked, "You brought a dog here?" "Nah." "Oh, that's for dude in the basement". He just looked at Quincey giving him a quizzical look that was ignored for what should have been obvious, he hit the switch to the basement light and entered. He found Benjamin asleep on the floor so he walked over and clapped both of his hands together making a loud thunderous sound causing Benjamin to jerk being as though he didn't have any wiggle room to jump up. "Ah...there is my friend, I couldn't just let you starve, so I brung you something I thought you'd like". Benjamin's vision was blurred, his sugar was low, and he was light headed so he really couldn't see the letters on the can to know it was dog food, nor did he like the idea of eating out of a can, but he hadn't eaten in a couple of days and the pain he was feeling from the stomach cramps was becoming intolerable. Quincey cut the tape around his mouth causing a jolt of pain to shoot through Benjamin's jaw where he had been hit with the mallet. "My bad, I'll try to be careful the next time", he said dumping the content from the can onto the basement floor and said, "I'm a love watching this, enjoy my friend". Benjamin's dignity and self-respect was literally standing between him and his dog food on the floor. Quincey became irate, rose up and turned into another person Jeff had never seen before. "Oh...you too good to eat the shit I paid for out of my pocket?" On the other hand, in order for Benjamin to at least have a fighting chance, he would have to eat to allow himself to place some energy into his body, and once the opportunity presented itself, he was going to pay Quincey back all that he owed him. Quincey walked over to the toolbox looking for a sharp object. "Bingo!" He stormed over to Benjamin and grabbed him by the back of the collar like one would grab his dog for using the bathroom on the carpet, forced his face down in the dog food, place the sharp pointed object to the hole of Benjamin's ear and said, "Bitch eat! Now I done spared ya mutha fucking ass far too long. Then...you got the mutha fucking nerve to be ungrateful after all...bitch, eat!" Benjamin was trying to breathe and get through the pain all at the same time while trying to eat from off the floor. "I don't hear yoe mutha fucking teeth chomping". He started pushing the sharp pointed object down in Benjamin's ear. The sounds he made trying to eat off the floor sounded like someone trying to drink soda through a straw that was no longer in the cup.

Jeff sat there trying to figure out who was this mad man who used to be his friend. Jeff started to think to himself, "should all black people be this angry?" The whole time they were driving, neither said a word except when he dropped Quincey off. Quincey decided that he didn't want to go home just yet, so he started to roam around the neighborhood and stumbled on a police officer who was responding to a disturbance that could have possibly been a domestic violence situation. When the officer learnt that it was a false alarm, he kept poking the bear attempting to get the guy who was still standing on his porch, to play right his hand just so he could make the arrest that he came for. "Won't you go head and leave, you see ain't nothing going on here, won't you go to your job", the guy yelled at the officer becoming more and more agitated as the officer continued to provoke the man. "You say one more thing, and I'm taking you in for disorderly conduct". "Man...get the..." "That's it, put your hands behind your back". "You can't be serious", Quincey said to himself, "I guess that's how they provide jobs for the generations to come". He eased over by the back of the car, pulled the face mask out of his pocket and put it on. Soon as the cop opened the door to place his detainee in the back seat, he was blindsided with a hard right hand to the jaw. He tried to turn in the direction that the punch came from, and was kicked hard in the back of the knee causing a loud cracking sound. The cop let out a painful shriek, and no sooner than it ended, Quincey had the cop's gun. He caught the handcuff key and signaled for the detainee to move back, he pointed the gun down on top of the cop's cranium, and squeezed the trigger. *Boom!* "Oh, shit", the detainee said jumping away from Quincey as he was trying to remove the cuff from the other wrist. Quincey threw the key on the ground and disappeared. The detainee looked over at his girlfriend who was still standing on the porch stunned. *"Bitch you better dial 9-1-1! Matter of fact, dial 9-1-1, cuff me back up, and sit me right there in that backseat…. shit… I won't be going to jail for murdering a cop today".* His girlfriend went to walk off, *"Bitch…shut the door, Out ya gotdamn mind…you tryna help me go to jail!"*

It looked as if every cop car in the city was present at the crime scene almost instantly, the officer asking questions seemed to be confused and frustrated at the same time, because the more he asked the detainee what happened, he kept making everything about his self. "Now again...I'm trying to find out what happened to the dead officer here, not you". *"I told you, he was fuckin' wit me 'bout a fake disorderly conduct...or some shit...and, boom".* "Gotdammit! Get this idiot away from me". They tried prying information from the girlfriend who could only be helpful for three sentences to wrap up the whole saga. *"They was arresting my man for nothing. I heard a shot. And whoever that was, took off".* "So ma'am you didn't see a face, he didn't say anything, was he African American..."? *"No, and who said anything about a him, and why every criminal got to be black"?* "Get both of them the hell out of here", the detective said knocking on other doors trying to find somebody who may of saw something. They harassed the area for hours looking for the would be suspect who they were having a hard time tracking. Quincey made it in safely through his window, picked up a pen and his notebook, and continued from where he left off the last time he wrote. He finished a few paragraphs or so, and relaxed on his bed as if he was lying in a coffin with his eyes wide open. His thoughts were processing rapidly, and his mind was more exhilarating then it had been but he didn't seem to be in a cheerful mind state. All he kept thinking about was the final hour.

CHAPTER 3

Jeff was sitting in his room playing the game when his father called him downstairs. "Coming", when Jeff really had no plans on leaving his room anytime soon. He spent hundreds of hours trying to get to the next phase, and now that he was finally there, he didn't want to be bothered. He had been so engaged in the video game, he didn't know that his father was standing in the doorway. "Did you not hear me calling you son?" He spoke in a real calm voice until what he heard in reply. "Yeah, I heard you, soon as I clear this level, I'll be down". "You ungrateful sonofabitch", he grabbed the controller from Jeff's hands with such brutal force, it caused Jeff to rise up. "What?" His father threw the controller in to the TV screen as hard as he could, it left the controller stuck in the screen. "What is it you want, you don't even talk to me any other time unless we got company, what?" "You little dip shit, I'll talk to you any gotdamn time I feel like it, or whenever the hell I get good and ready to!" He threw Jeff so hard into the wall, it left a gigantic hole. Jeff stood up straight and balled his fist up, staring his father down. He knew his dad was drunk, but he wasn't about to take the abuse that his mother had been taking since he was born. *"Oh, so you're a man now, that's what your implying boy, you wanna piece of the old man huh? Well let's have it".* Jeff charged at him, stopped on a dime and threw a punch, his martial arts weren't the best as he was still learning so he only knew what all Quincey had been teaching him. His father moved to the side as if he saw that same punch one too many times before. When Jeff started sailing by, he grabbed Jeff's throat pulling him backwards, wrapped his forearm around his neck, placed his other hand on the side of Jeff's hand and started squeezing. Jeff tried desperately to shake loose but couldn't. He then tried to elbow his father in the stomach, but the old man seemed to be solid. Fighting for oxygen, he heard his dad say something about him knowing where Ben had gone. He had one option left, so he took it. He reached down and grabbed what he believed to be the groin and squeezed for dear life. When he left the vise around his neck loosen, he spun around watching his dad drop to the floor like a sack of potatoes. His uncaged years worth of rage he had kept locked up, finally been released. With every punch he threw, he explained why it had to land, and by the time Jeff had grown tired and exhausted, he sat on the bed while his dad layed on the floor balled up like a baby whimpering repeating that he was sorry. Jeff wasn't even thinking about the fact that his father had just tried to choke him out, but the fact that he said something about Benjamin.

Jeff found his phone buried under the pillows on his bed and sent a text to Quincey. "Me and my dad just went off". His dad had gotten up off of the floor as Jeff was responding back to Quincey's text and said, *"I want you out of this house, you hear me?"* He walked off when Jeff didn't respond. All of a sudden Jeff heard his mother's voice not knowing exactly when it was that she entered the house, but sure enough, it sounded like an argument between both of the parents. When Jeff walked down the stairs, all he saw was his father's hand raised high in the air coming down hard across his mother's cheek. *Wham! "This is my house, and I say who stays..."* Jeff ran full speed and jumped up into a spinning kick that brought his dad down hard. He dove on him with a passion to destroy him with an abundance of blows as if his life depended on it. *"I will kill you"*, he kept yelling the whole time his mother was trying to pull him away. *"Please Jeff, please honey, it's okay"*.

But her cry was never heard as Jeff kept pounding his father away. When he finally withdrew from punishing his father, he realized that he wasn't moving. *His mother kept saying, "Get up Jimmy, come on baby just get up. He didn't mean it, he's your son baby, come on Jimmy...baby, please get up".* Jeff didn't know why he was calling 911, as far as he was concerned, he could of laid right there on the floor until somebody else came and cleaned him up for all the pain and misery that he brought in to the house that was supposed to be home for them.

When the police had arrived at the residence, his mother was still laying on his father's chest begging that he get up. The homicide detectives had a hard time pulling Jeff's mother away from her dead husband, but finally succeed. When they asked what happened, Jeff took them all the way back to when it initially started. *"So he had been drinking from your recollection?"* the first homicide detective questioned. *"yes sir, then he became highly upset because I didn't come right away when he called. The guy attacked me"*, he said showing them the hole in his bedroom wall. *"And then what happened?"* asked detective number two. *"He told me he wanted me out, and he left out, but as I was coming downstairs I saw him attacking my mom. I only came down when I heard them arguing about me leaving, he's always been abusive. But when I saw him attacking my mom like that, you see how small she is, I just reached, not to seriously hurt him, but to make him stop".* Jeff was trying to think quickly to prevent them from arresting him, he said, *"I think this was all about his friend that he wanted to stay here and told me not to say anything to anybody".* *"And who might that friend be?"* The first detective asked not believing the story would really go anywhere. *"Some guy he said he knew for years that I never saw, named Benjamin Taggart or something like that, but I believe that was it".* Everything else was out the window when the detectives heard the name. "Have you actually seen this Benjamin guy?" *"They were in the basement one day, just a couple of days ago drinking when he called me down to meet him and told me to not say anything to anyone".* "A, Jackson, can you come up here for a minute?" Detective one yelled down the steps. "Yeah, this kid here, says that Benjamin Taggart was right here in the basement a few days ago and the old man told him not to say anything to anyone. Show the kid a picture and see if that's the right one". Jeff looked at the picture from the detective's phone and said, *"Yeah that's him...uh huh, I'm pretty sure".* "A, this is detective Jackson from homicide, and I am here at 24S, 19th street where we are investing an accidental homicide involving a teenager who says that

Benjamin Taggart was right here at this address no longer than a few days ago, could you have agent Cooper give me a call...yeah, he has my number. Thank you". "Well listen", said detective one. "I don't see no real reason to take the kid down for questioning, his story checks out, I mean there's no doubt as to whether or not the old man was drunk or not, whole bottle of whisky almost empty down there on the dining room table. See this here hole in the wall, kid said he pushed'em into it, looks more like he threw'em into it. There aren't no real situation that looks like the house was ram sacked and then they tried to make it fit the story". "It's typical protocol, I would take'em down", detective Jackson said walking off.

Detective two just shrugged his shoulders and said, "It's your call". "Well...there's no need, I mean it's not like he's some black kid from out of the ghetto or anything like that, cause then we'd have to be worried. I mean those kids kill for no reason at all", he said walking off, "I'm just gonna go downstairs and wait for the mother to pull it together so we can wrap this up. That Jackson nigger got some nerve huh?" Detective two just nodded and agreed with everything being said, then looked back at Jeff and said, "go back to whatever you were doing kid". Jeff listened to the detectives just speak in such a way as if he wasn't even standing there. He was beginning to understand everything that Quincey was pointing out in most of their conversations where he would always talk about how a lot of Europeans thought that things were supposed to go the way in which they saw fit. He went down stairs to comfort his mother, watching detective one, the whole time attempt to get everybody to leave so that he didn't have to do his job. When everybody was out of the house, Jeff put his mother in her car and took her over to his aunt Laura's house, explained the situation as best he could and left. He knew his mother's sister could not stand to even be in the same room as his father, so she rarely went to visit.

Jeff called Quincey soon as he got in his mom's car, *"Where you at bro?...Meet me outside in about fifteen minutes"*. By the time he pulled into a parking space, he was shocked to see Quincey standing near the bumper of the car once he looked up. *"you wanna ride or walk"*, Quincey said observing the newer model BMW he hadn't seen before. Jeff didn't get out of the vehicle so Quincey already figured the obvious and got in. "How come I never saw this one before? I wouldn't leave it parked here either, they wouldn't mess with it though". Jeff exited the car, and soon as Quincey got out he locked the door and actuated the alarm. They strolled the neighborhood where Jeff started to fill Quincey in on everything that happened from the time his dad had pushed him into the wall. Quincey looked at Jeff and stopped walking and said, *"Damn, I can't even begin to imagine what you must be going through, I mean, I know you didn't have much of a relationship with your dad, but it's your mother I'm worried about, the only two men in her life she loved, and the one she give birth to, took it away, the one who helped her conceive. That's deep".* "Yeah, my mom", was all Jeff could say verbally although his mind was painting a perfect picture of pretty much everything he wanted to say. *"So what you wanna do, you know my place is pretty much yours if you don't care to stay at home, but what you plan to do about your mom?" "I dropped her off over my aunt's, she'll call when she's ready for me to come and get her, I doubt she wanna look at my face, I mean you had to see how she dove on him telling him to get up like he didn't just strike her with such heavy force". "Well you know what they say, love conquers all". "I just wanna ride for a minute, I really wanna let off some steam". "You know what they say, never let anger cloud your judgement...whole lot of truth to that".* Jeff decided to drive to his house, so he and Quincey entered and went straight to his room where he showed him the damage his dad had done to his TV and wall. *"And you said that's because you didn't get up right away when he called you?" "Yeah, but he was mumbling something about that Benjamin dude in the basement, he stopped talking when he challenged me to a fight". "I've been thinking". "What's that?" "Of letting dude clean up a little, cause that smell be killing me". "Well you the one who left him down there to begin with". "I think this time I'll take him some sweats, get'em some hygiene products, and this time some cat food". "Are you serious?" Jeff asked. "All this happening is because of him. Everything!"* His voice raised up a few notches. *"Trevon's dead, cause of him...all of them cops dead...cause of him...is because of him. Everything! Now when he's no longer of any use to me, that's when it's over. The same way they play God when they lock my people up for pretty crimes or crimes they hadn't committed, and give'em a hundred years and play God! I am God to him, fuck'em!" "I see what you saying, but you got to calm down and chill out, you letting your judgment be clouded". "That bitch is still alive cause I'm calm. Matter of fact, let's go there so you can see if he think I'm angry".* They stopped at the dollar general and picked up the necessary items, and then headed to the basement where Benjamin layed. Benjamin was wide awake when the two came in the door sounding as if they had brought company for him. He never endured such torture in his entire life or time of living and now just wished that he was dead to alleviate the troubles yet to come. To his surprise, when they cut on the light, they came down with two buckets, and then went to retrieve a few bags they returned with. *"Guess today's your lucky day my friend. I am going to cut you loose and allow you to clean yourself, please, do not, and I repeat, do not try to rein-act these things that you may have seen on TV. Keep it simple"*. Jeff took the razor and cut straight down the tape not even caring if he cut Benjamin by accident or not. When Jeff got the tape off the upper half of Benjamin's body, he left the rest up to him to get off, trying to avoid the smell of feces and urine. Both buckets contained soap and water, he was handed a wash cloth a towel, a pair of depends underwear, and some sweats. Benjamin turned to look at them with a facial expression that said, *"Are you really gonna watch me?"* Quincey noticed the expression almost right away, and laughed for a minute. *"You really believe this is TV I see. See the way you think, that come from being the wrong kind of European. If things happened like TV, you probably wouldn't be in this predicament that you're in now. See how thinking like you're on TV got you?"* Benjamin finished washing, dried off and got dressed looking to seize his opportunity. He attempted to pick up the buckets and walk them over to Jeff and Quincey. *"Nah, you can put them back, ain't nobody tell you to take them nowhere bruh"*. When he went to sit them down, he quickly lifted a bucket to throw on Quincey and Jeff, and made a run for it. Quincey already anticipated what just unfolded to happen no sooner than he tried it. They still got splashed a little, jumping out of the way, trying to regroup as Benjamin tried to make a run for it. All Benjamin saw trying to run up the steps, were those same steps closing in on his face when he was tased. He layed there flopping like a fish on land as Jeff kept on squeezing the trigger laughing. *"I know what you thinking, or thought, that's right"*, he said to Jeff, *"drag his monkey ass back over there"*. He started taping up Benjamin's legs then his arms. He took one of Benjamin's old socks, and balled it up, and then started stuffing it in his mouth after he wiped it with the same water that had feces residue floating around in, and wrapped the tape around twice. *"See, you thought that if you didn't succeed in ya TV escape, that somebody might kill ya sorry ass. Nope, it's always a good day to die, just not today"*. *"I'll be back for you real soon"*, Jeff said taking off his shirt throwing it at Benjamin to believe that they weren't coming back, so he finally gave in and quit fighting and went right out. He was snoring when they returned and didn't even hear them come down the steps. When he opened his eyes he thought to his self that there was wither two statuses in the house, it was a dream, or somebody was picking on him. When he tried to turn out of the way since he couldn't move directly out of the line of fire, they peed on his face and hair. Jeff felt that now was a good time as any, to finally release his frustrations, so he went from peeing to kicking Benjamin. *"Absolutely, everybody should feel this way when dealing with a piece of shit. Fuck him up, I encourage you, do him!"* Quincey yelled trying to inspire Jeff to release, *"Get it all out"*. The punishment seemed a bit much so he grabbed him, *"Alright, that's enough my boy, you got what needed to get. Let's go, it's over"*. Jeff was crying so Quincey knew it had to be the drama with his own family that was the cause of this stress. *"You sure you gonna, be alright?"* Quincey injured with one foot out of the car. *"I'm good now"*, Jeff responded, but then asked, *"When, or what do you plan to do with my man in the basement?"* *"I would tell you, but you would only interfere as a friend. I love you like my own brother, and you've done enough, but this one is on me man...go ahead and live ya life bruh"*. *"I thought we..."*

"And we accomplished what needed to be accomplished. The plan wasn't even for you to be this deeply involved, but you were. This is my journey from here on out, I may need your help with some minor things, but mainly from the background so I know for sure everything is handled correctly". He looked at Jeff and said, *"There can't be any room for any errors; most importantly"*. Jeff nodded, giving him a pound and drove off. Quincey walked in the house rushing to his room to get out of his clothes. Once he was done he grabbed his pen and pad, and started to write again getting deeper into it.

CHAPTER 4

When he got within rage, he could now hear what was going on. *"I told you I ain't nobody's boy, I stopped being that at the age of twenty one. Now I'm trying to be respectful even though ya'll the one's who are wrong as usual. I'm done with it, I got to be to work, can I get there?"* "Now see there boy!", the officer emphasized the word boy and continued, *"you just committed verbal assault on a police officer, and you keep giving me ya lip, I might just have to take you in. What you think partner?"* *"Man I'm trying to leave, what the fuck is you talkin' bout. What you think partner, who does that? Then this miserable cracka too busy dick riding ya sorry ass cause he probably don't know how to do his own job..."* *"That's enough, that's it, place your hands behind your back"*. Quincey stepped right on in as if on cue, *"Is there a problem with my uncle or something?"* he let them see he was recording the incident, but the fact that they remembered his face from the incident involving Trevon, they started to back off and get in their squad car. Soon as they were gone, the older black guy said, *"Thanks young blood, what's ya name?"* *"Quincey"* *"Them pigs there, I ain't got it to do. I would of went to jail and ended up losing my job, all for nothing. They roll up, I'm tryna get in my car, and they start accusing me of being somebody I look nothing like. Ain't this bout a.....".* Quincey shook the man's hand and went on his way proud he could help. That incident only fueled the fire that had been burning since day one. During lunch break, Quincey showed Jeff the video from earlier. *"I told you it never stops. This is why this has to happen, either people are really crazy, or they really believe what they are doing is right. Now one way on the other, I'm a fix that."*

"How are you today Ms. Fallings?" "I'm fine, and you?" "Could be better, but whose complaining?" "I guess you know why I'm calling". "Well I hope it's good news". "I haven't heard anything, I was hoping you knew something that may have been helpful". "Alright then agent Cyrus". Stacy felt that the system was ridiculous where they would bug someone's life for years, but can't find somebody living practically next door. She then tried calling detective Atkins but got no answer. She thought, what the hell, why not try his house one more time. Stacy got out the car, looked around, and noticed that Hector's car was still parked in the same place she saw it in the last time she came by. She knocked on the door still unable to get a response until she turned to walk away did she hear a small voice say, *"Yes, may I help you?"* It was Hector's wife who acknowledged Stacy once she turned around. *"Oh hi. If I would have known that you were home, I would have been stopped by. How are you and the children?",* she asked wondering if Hector's wife knew he may be missing. *"Mrs. DeJesus, may I come in for a brief minute and speak to you about your husband?" "Please, call me Maria",* she said moving to the side to let Stacy in. She offered some refreshments soon as Stacy was seated. *"No thank you Maria, I wanted to ask you if you saw or heard from Hector within the last few days or so?" "Actually I was worried, reason why I came back home. He called to let me know that he was coming home, he gave me the code to the alarm system he had installed, said to give it a few days to make sure it was safe before me and the kids were to come home".* She let out a deep sigh, struggled and said, *"I don't know, he would never just up and go without saying anything". "I, along with special Agent Cyrus, and Detective Atkins and hadn't gotten a answer. So I'll let you know if he's heard anything, here, take my number",* Stacy offered. Stacy excused herself and left hoping she would have heard back from detective Atkins by now, but she didn't so she thought she should just go home and wait for any

kind of news.

Quincey decided that today would be the day, that he go and visit Cindy feeling guilty that he hadn't been to visit her but one time on his own since Trevon's death. He knocked on the door and was surprised that she answered on the first knock. *"Ah...you're home"*, *"Well it's mine, and besides, I ain't got nowhere else to be"*, she said extending her arms for a hug. *"Come on in here boy"*, she said smiling, *"What you doing, tryna' check up on ol' auntie, look at you"*. *"I should have been coming by more often, I just been trying to keep myself busy is all. Everything's just different now"*. *"I know what you mean, I even find myself cleaning his room, but you know...what can we do"*, she shrugged, *"It will eventually pass"*. In an instant, Quincey became that vulnerable that he just laid his head on Cindy's shoulder. *"I know"*, she whined, *"It'll be alright baby"*. She broke into a cheerful spirit, *"Now tell me what you been up to since you've been keeping yourself busy, I know you got a little girlfriend?"* *"I talk to her every now and then"*, he said smiling, *"too much work on my plate"*. *"you make sure you stay focus, and remember..."* *"I know... plenty of time to play later"*. *"That's my nephew. Boy you getting a little swoll what you been doing?"* she said feeling his bicep. *"I've been training in mixed martial arts"*, *"Okay, I see you neph"*. After about a good two hour chat, Quincey got up to leave saying that he would be by tomorrow to see her, said his good-byes and left.

Jeff sat in the living room with his mom trying to explain that he didn't mean what happened with his father to accept it as an accident so she could calm her nerves since she was feeling like the only way to do that, was to drink. *"Jeff I am not having this conversation with you young man"*. *"Mom you have to, it's the only way we're gonna get passed it. How could you allow yourself to believe that I could be so malice. My own mom"*. He got up to walk away when she stopped him. *"Wait Jeff, I'm sorry honey, it's just that...I don't know anyone, he's the only man I ever been with since prom...the only man I ever loved"*. *"I get it mom, he was my father, but you are gonna have to get on with your life, I will be here for you, we still have each other"*. *"I know Jeffy"*, she said getting up to give him a hug. *"We'll be alright mom"*, he took her glass and poured it in the sink feeling as if she had too much to drink already and asked, *"Are you hungry?"* *"No honey, I'm alright, I'll just lie down for a while"*. *"You have to eat something"*. *"No, no, I'll be alright"*. Jeff brought his hand down on the table hard causing his mother to jump. *"Your gonna hit me too Jeff, is that your answer for everything?"* *"No. No one is gonna hit you"*, his voice went up not really yelling, *"but you have to stop acting as if life is over!"* *"Why are you yelling at me Jeff, I am your mother?"* Jeff knew he wasn't going to get anywhere while she was intoxicated, so he thought better to not argue and said, *"Yeah, come on, I think you should lie down for a while"*. She agreed and went up to her room to retire for the night.

Quincey called Diamond, she was the girl he was talking to, a close friend, who told Trevon's mother about the video her friend Mariah had recorded of the cop killing her son. Quincey hadn't really been taking any calls from anyone, or being on social media for that matter. She picked up immediately recognizing his picture light up on the screen of her phone. *"Hey stranger, hadn't talked or seen you in a while except for school, did I do something to you?"* She giggled for a while and then waited for him to respond. *"I've been extra busy lately, I wasn't ducking you, and no you didn't do anything wrong"*. *"Well where you at, I wanna see you?"* she whined. *"I was just leaving my aunt's house, the one whose house you brought Mariah over that day. I hadn't really been to see her in a while either"*. *"So I guess you was just checkin' on me cause you miss me huh?"* *"Actually I do, I called you, did I not?"* *"Well when you gonna come see me?"*

"That depends". "Stop playing", she continued to whine. Quincey didn't say anything for a while when Diamond broke the silence and said, *"My mom is still on vacation and won't be back for another week and I've been here by myself, is you gonna come and keep me company?" "Give me a few minutes cause I'm a walk over there, I need some air". "You ain't coming..." "Promise, I rather walk right now, just clearing my head, that's all, I'll be there girl". "I'll be out front then".*

Quincey decided to make a quick stop at the mini mart to grab a few things, including condoms, feeling like this may be his best opportunity to not only have sex with Diamond, but to make love to her if there was really such a thing for teenagers. *"Yeah, give me the extra thin ones...the pack of three".* It took all about fifteen minutes to get there, and once Diamond saw Quincey turn the corner looking all sexy, biting his bottom lip, she literally jumped from the porch into his arms. *"Quincy",* she sang, *"hi honey, I didn't think you was coming"* he hugged her hard and long to answer her question. *"Come on",* she said tugging his hand leading him into the house, *did you eat yet baby?"* Not really waiting on a response she asked him, *"what would you like me to fix you baby?" "It don't matter, don't put yourself through no extra trouble". "I got you baby".*

She pulled out a sir loin steak, tenderized it, seasoned it, and then dropped it in a non-stick pan with some olive oil. She poured white rice into a pot and pulled some broccoli out of the freezer to stream once the rice was done. She sat on Quincey's lap in between time just staring into his light brown eyes. *"Tell me what you miss about me?" "Boy you better stop playin' wit me, you know I miss everything about you",* she said swatting his chest with the dish towel as she was getting up to go check on the food again. She made his plate, put the napkin over his lap, placed her hand underneath her chin and watched him eat. Once he was finished, she cleaned the dishes while chatting with him. *"Do you have time for a movie?" "Yeah, I suppose"*. She already had the comforter out while she was laying on the sectional watching TV. She got underneath and threw the comforter over the both of them.

Quincey let out a slight chuckle when he saw the romantic movie start playing on the screen. Mid way through the movie, Diamond looked up at Quincey and was surprised that he was deep in the movie, so she let him finish the movie. Once the movie was over, she turned the TV station to a slow R&B vibe, tossed the remote control on the coffee table and straddled Quincey tracing the outlines of his lips with her tongue. *"I really miss you daddy"*, she begin to moan kissing the tip of his nose, then she slipped her tongue into his mouth savoring the taste of his tongue. She withdrew her tongue and started sticking it in his ear. She sat erect and took off her shirt, freed her breast from her bra feeling pure ecstasy, she slid all the way to the floor reaching for the buckle of his belt unbuckling it. Once she unbuttoned his pants, she yanked them down feeling the hunger. She removed his dick from his boxer briefs and attempted to devour the whole shaft. It felt so good that he let out a sound that even he was unfamiliar with and held on to the couch for dear life. Diamond was working the rim of his dick in two ways Quincey never knew existed. She was making slurping sounds sucking as if she was possessed in a demonic state. He was about to feel heaven on earth from raw bliss, but he didn't want to spill his fluids into her mouth, so he tried to pry her face from his penis and was unsuccessful and she greedily swallowed everything. It took approximately two full minutes for his toes to uncurl. Soon as he gained his energy, he pulled up his pants and scooped her up carrying her to her bedroom. He tossed her on the bed and stripped off his and the rest of her clothes. He crawled in between her legs kissing the inside of her thighs, he slid down lifting up one leg at a time kissing the back of her knees. He crawled back up, but this time to her breast showing precise attention. They were soft and delicate, delectable at its best. *"Mmmmm...that's my spot"*, she cried as her body shook, *"Oooh...ba...by"*. He slid back in between her legs to return the favor. He wrote the alphabet in capital and lower case letters twice causing her to scratch both sides of his shoulders when her body started convulsing. *"Please put it in"*, she cried. Although she was a virgin, she didn't care about the pain her friends spoke about their first time. Quincey went to reach for the condoms and she stopped him, *"No, I trust you baby"*, she whispered. *"Please"*. He climbed on top, having no idea that she was that wet, he slid all the way in and the state of mind she was in, she didn't feel any of the pain her girl friends spoke of. *"Ooooh...rig...ht...there ba...by. Yess, I love you Quincey"*. He attempted to say it back but got cut off mid way about to erupt. *"I'm about to..."* *"Baby don't move, please don't move, right there, that's the spot. My...sp..ot. Oooo oooh"*. They climbed together, after Diamond was able to regroup, she told him to lie on his back and she straddled him. She began to ride him in a rhymic flow like she were dancing to an exotic beat. *"Ooh"*, she cooed. Neither wanted this night to end, she just kept cumin then said, *"fuck me from the back...and don't you waste a drop...shoot it all in me, fuck me hard daddy"*. Quincey didn't know what had gotten into her, but he had no complaints. When they finished they laid there cuddling until Diamond spoke up for the first time since the last position. *"Baby, I know you keep saying you was busy, but you got me thinking somebody else is trying steal my spot"*, she said playfully, *"nah, what's really bothering you, you wanna talk about it?"* *"Trust me, I would, but it's not something you can just put into words or I would have been spoke on it"*. *"You sound heart broken, come here and let Diamond fix it"*. She rolled over on top of him kissing the area where his heart was located, and then started to perform oral sex again. This time she looked up at him when he was about to cum and just as he released his load in her mouth, she saw a tear roll down his cheek. She thought that it was from the best oral sex he'd ever had, but it was everything. His mind was already made up and he felt guilty as to who and what he would leave behind. For one, he may not even see his father get vindicated and freed from prison.

Two, he loved his mother and siblings with an undying love, and know the pain it would cause once he left the earth. Not to mention his grandparents on either side, then there was her, Diamond, somebody he wanted to spend the rest of his life with. None of them deserved that, but in this life, sometimes you have to be selfish to accomplish things that are important, or for self-gratification. In his case, he felt it was very important, and so it shall be done. He just laid there staring at the ceiling holding Diamond close to his chest. When she was sound asleep he carefully wiggled his way from underneath her, kissed her on the forehead, crept down the steps, locked the door behind him and left out.

Quincey hadn't even paid attention to it being curfew when he bent the corner and saw the police. Soon as they hit the sirens, he took off running, but everywhere he turned, another car was there as if they knew where he was going. Soon as he got near an alley way and ended up in the middle of it, they blocked off both ends of the streets. He didn't think it'd be wise to reach for his hands up. When the first two officers approached him, he recognized them immediately from the other day on his way to school when they were out harassing the man from his neighborhood. *"Ah, thought you'd never see up again, huh boss?" "See you for what?" "Don't play that game with me, you remember what you did"*. Quincey didn't feed into it, he just stood there.

"You got some I.D. boy?" "No sir". "And where do you think you were going at this time of night?" "Home". "Probably out starting some trouble, all you black sons of bitches are always looking for trouble. "Go search-'em Dave", they flicked a flashlight in his eyes as if the lights from the squad car wasn't bright enough. Soon as Quincey blocked the light from his eyes, the officers became excited, "Oh, we got one resisting". No sooner than the words left his mouth, there was at least ten officers jumping Quincey in the alley way hitting him with night-sticks, spraying him with mace, stomping and kicking him. Quincey phone started to ring, it was his mom calling. He struggled to answer while the officers continued to swoop him. When he finally answered his cellphone his mom could hear the officers' beating her son. She screamed, *"I know ya'll better get ya fuckin' hands off that one if you know what's best!* "Quincey", she yelled. *"Mom".* He coughed, wheezing from the possibility of having fractured ribs. *"Hold on baby, I'm coming".* The cops just left him in the alleyway as if nothing ever happened going on about their day. Karmen pulled up Quincey's location on her phone and followed the directions. When she pulled up in a small alleyway that the GPS directed her to, she was more hysterical than shocked to see her baby to whom she gave birth to, fighting to stand on his own two feet. She pulled just mid-way through the alley to help him with a stream of tears rolling down her face. *"Mommy got you",* she said trying to breathe through the heavy scent of the mace the officers repeatedly sprayed Quincey with. Karmen jumped on the highway to get to the hospital the quickest way possible. When she pulled up right in front of the entrance, she jumped out and ran into the hospital yelling to the lady behind the glass that it was an emergency. While Karmen paced back and forth in the waiting room, she kept mumbling to herself, *"somebody tell me something. Please oh please God let my baby be alright".* She picked up her

cellphone from off one of the small tables that they kept there magazines on and sent a text to KJ's phone letting him know that she might need an attorney for her son. Just as soon as she went back to pacing, a doctor bust through the double doors yelling for a Ms. Whitaker. *"Is there a Ms. Whitaker..."* *"Right here"*, she waved looking desperate. *"How are you today Ms...."* *"No, please...is my baby alright, is he okay?"* she started to panic. *"Yes, please take a seat, he's just fine. He suffered two fractured ribs and a bruised lung. But he should be fine in maybe a month, and he has a little swelling on the face".* *"Can I see my baby, where he..."* *"Right this way Ms. Whitaker".* He led her through the doors directly to Quincey's room. She was damn near in tears again when her eyes set upon him seeing her child propped up looking so innocent but hurt. In her mind, no mother should ever feel this way.

"Hi baby". *"Hmmm"* *"Are you okay?"* *"I'm alright".* Just as he finished, Karmen started chastising him.

"Didn't I tell you to be careful out there? You got me all scared and carrying on, boy what happened?" *"Nothing..."* *"Don't tell me nothing, you was lying in a alley way..."* *"You ain't let me finish"....* *"I was leaving from aunt Cindy's and ended up walking on the hill to go see Diamond, cause I hadn't talked to her in a while. We ate and watched a movie, I went to sleep and woke up and left not even knowing what time it was".* *"Yea, you probably did more than just ate, watched a movie and went to the sleep".* *"It was the same cops I saw the other day on my way to school harassing the old head from row 12 accusing him of looking like somebody else. I started recording asking was it a problem with my uncle, and they left. Soon as I turned the corner coming out of Diamond's house, it was like I felt somebody following me, but soon as I took off running, it was like they knew where I was already going and cut me off blocking both ends of the alleyway. It might have been ten of'em at least".*

"Well I'm going to talk to somebody about..." "Just let it go mom..." "Let nothing go..." "I got it mom, plus I got them on video from the other day and that CBS chick said she would love to have me on anytime". "You got it, you better, cause they fuckin' wit the wrong one now. Got me cussing and stuff. And boy you better be glad that you already hurt". "You can go home mom, I'll be fine once they discharge me, cause I know you got to get the twins ready for school". "Don't tell me what I got to do, I'm the mother, yeah, I'll be right back".

Quincey picked up the hospital phone and called Diamond to let her know he wouldn't be to school, and the reason why. Then he called Jeff to let him know what happened. Jeff cancelled his plans on going to school and went to the hospital instead to make sure his friend was alright. When he got there, he by passed the desk like he had already been where he was about to go so the lady at the desk didn't start to interrogate him about whether or not he was family. He made his way to the room that Quincey had gave him and walked in. *"What's up bro, what the hell happened man? I see I can't leave you by yourself for too long". "Nah bruh, I was on my way home when I ran into the cops from yesterday. I stopped them from harassing somebody who didn't fit the description of the guy they claimed to have been looking for." "Anyway, they was following me coming from Diamond's and blocked me off in a alley way and rushed me". "You alright though, right?" "I got a few fractured ribs and a swollen cheek, nothing major. My lungs will be alright, I should be healed in a month or so".* As they were talking, Karmen made it back with Diamond tagging along. *"Hi Ms. Karmen, Diamond". "Hey Jeff, didn't expect to see you here this soon". "Well, I got to check my boy make sure he good".* Quincey looked at Diamond who had a gift in being beautiful and asked, *"Why you ain't at school?" "The same reason you ain't in school, I don't hear you asking Jeff why he ain't in school".* Karmen placed both hands on her hips waiting on either one to say something. They waited on Quincey's property to be returned, then left after he signed the discharge papers and went to his house. When they got in the door, Karmen went up to the bathroom to run some bath water for Quincey. *"Come on up here boy so you can get the rest of that pepper spray off you"*. When she got in the kitchen, she called Diamond in, *"Come on in here girl"*, she said pulling out some breakfast materials. *"Jeff you eat this morning?" "I had cereal". "Well I cook in here… girl what ya'll do last night?"* she nudged Diamond with a playful elbow. *"He ate, watched a movie, and went to sleep". "Girl don't be holding out, he stayed the night over there".* Diamond started to giggle like a little school girl guiding herself away. *"I was young before too, ya'll better be using protection unless you feel like you are responsible to be raising babies, while going to school". "Why you look at me like that",* Diamond said putting her head down in a shy, manner. *"Uh huh".* Karmen liked Diamond, she was without questions, gorgeous with a good head on her shoulders, and respectful.

When Quincey finally made it downstairs, they were finally able to sit at the table and eat. After Karmen said grace, she started small talk to see what everybody had been up to. *"So what you doing after school Jeff?" "Me?"* Jeff responded pointing to his self *"Boy you the only Jeff in the entire house".* They all broke out laughing. *"I was going to Dukes to play ball and study science, but I may have to hold off". "Why?"* Karmen put her fork back on the plate staring at Jeff. *"My dad just died a few days ago, and my mom is in a bad place". "Oh my, what happened baby?" "I was in my bedroom playing the game when my dad was calling me, but when I went to get up to see what he wanted, he was standing right there. So he's like you don't hear me calling you. Long story, he snatched the controller throwing it into the TV screen literally, so I asked why he do that, he ends up pushing me into the wall making a big hole. We get into it, he said he wanted me out, I go to get up and I heard my mom and dad downstairs arguing. He's always putting his hands on her..."* *"Oh my"*, Karmen added. *"Soon as I get to the bottom of the steps , he was slapping her hard. So I ran as fast as I could and kicked him, and I just lost it. As I was punching him, I hadn't realized that he wasn't moving, I didn't know". "Oh baby, are you holding up okay?" "I mean I'm alright, but because we didn't have a close relationship and I use to tell her to leave and stop letting him abuse her I don't care.But my mom thinks I am a horrible monster". "Well if you need to talk or need some advice, I'm here". "Thanks Ms. Karmen". "What about you Diamond?" "Well, I still might go to school, but my grandfather wants me to run his night dubs, it's like six of them but* they are all down South". *"Well that's nice that you have a plan B if you change your mind".* Karmen got up and started collecting the plates, Diamond rose to help when Karmen waved her off. *"I got it baby." "Yall gonna be alright, cause I'm about to leave for work?" "We cool mom".*

CHAPTER 5

(3 WEEKS LATER)

For the past three weeks, Quincey had been doing real intense breathing exercises while meditating. *"What did the doc say?"* Jeff inquired, *"He said I was coming along pretty good, especially for just three weeks". "Well yeah, cause we got to do something with him in the basement, like I've been feeding him and all that, but I know he had to come to some type of conclusion sitting there all that time". "Yeah you absolutely right so let me get on my game and start putting this together, but first, I want them two cops who jumped me. Find out when exactly they start their shift. I know they were out there when I went to school that morning, and it was like five or six in the morning when they jumped me". "Well we can always wait around by the station for them to change shifts and tail gate one of 'em, I'm sure one will lead you to the other". "No doubt, but we got to make sure they are on duty instead of just popping up looking out of place cause you know the courthouse is right across the street". "We got all night to figure it out cause we might be able to catch 'em early in the morning". "Well make sure you up then, and be dressed for the occasion".* They parked the van on the side of a house that sat on Sycamore Street, waiting to see if they could spot the two officers that they were scouting for. *"Bingo, I can spot him from anywhere!"*

Quincey got excited when he saw the cop he developed hate for. The squad car made a fatal mistake stopping in the street near the same area they were at when they were harassing the wrong man. Quincey let the drone, once it locked in its targets, do its job. The only problem was, once the drone fried both shots, only one was hit and that was the partner on the passenger side known as Dave. But the driver for some odd reason was hunched down or something, somewhere out of harms way. Quincey didn't want to waste any time, so he grabbed the pistol on the floor and said to Jeff, *"Put the drone in the van and meet me on Rolleston"*. He pulled his mask up and jumped out of the van and raced down the middle of the street and saw that the cop was busy trying to clean up the hot coffee he spilled on his self, that he hadn't even noticed that his partner was dead. Quincey wanted his attention so he opened the door and said, *"You'll figure it out the next time you see me"*. Boom! He hadn't even given the cop time to respond before the head shot. Quincey took off through the back rows and stayed within the housing area so he didn't come in contact with any other cops lurking in the cut unexpectedly, but he kept the gun out just in case. Quincey had already made up his mind that regardless of the situation, that he was going to his grave either in the process, or, after the mission was complete, but it had to be done. He came up on one of the rows by the Boys and Girls Club, tucked the pistol when he saw that it was clear, pulled off his mask and jogged across the street. By the time that he made it to Rolleston street, he could hear the sirens in the distance almost harmonious. He saw where Jeff was parked, he looked around and got in. *"Go out 19th way with the traffic"*, he reached in his pocket and pulled out his excuse note for the teacher for being late. They made it near the school, stashed the van, and walked the rest of the way. When they made it inside the building the period was changing so they fit right in where the students were all exchanging greetings. When school was out, Quincey had made a necessary decision to go to the gym since he had been put of real physical commission. After a real intense workout he spoke briefly with his trainer and then left headed home, showered, ate, and then spent time with his family. After a few lessons of chess with his siblings, he then went over to his Aunt Cindy's for a while. She already knew that he was coming, so she left the door unlocked so he could just come on in. *"Hey nephew"*, she called from the kitchen. *"What's that you cooking?" "You don't know nothin' bout this. Boy that's liver, gravy, and rice. See, the fried onions bring all this to life. Your mom don't cook this?" "Yeah, but I don't eat it". "Cause you hear the name and think negative, trust me baby, your hard headed daddy was like that growing up, and then found out he was missing something very exquisite". "Anyway, it sounds good..." "Don't knock it until you try it". "I'm a see what all this hype is about". "That's what I'm talking bout nephew, give me some"*, she raised her hand in the air to give Quincey five. When the food was done, she made Quincey a whole plate. *"Nah, I didn't want all of that". "Nobody tries it and then don't want anymore. You want water or something else?" "Water is cool. Thank you". "Your welcome, and then your welcome for after you are finished, cause you are going to thank me".*

Before Cindy knew it, Quincey devoured the whole plate scraping what residue that was left if any. *"Boy give me that plate"*, she said grabbing the empty plate and refilling it. *"Here, take your time with this one".* They laughed and then Quincey said, *"Oh, you got jokes huh? "Well if that was a question, it don't deserve my time in answering it".* They finished, he helped her with the dishes and then they went into the living room. *"So what's good wit you?" "All ain't nothing, just handling my business". "Your mom just told me what happened to you, I don't know why she waited this long". "Cause I asked her not to. I mean you still dealing with Trevon's situation, and my dad with his, and my mom trying to find time to be there for everybody else, I don't want to be a burden..." "A burden",* she cut him off, *"I do understand what you mean, but you are still the child in this instance. Don't be making no decisions for us, let us do the worrying and what not".* He got up indicating that he was getting ready to leave, *"Let me get ready to start my journey"*, he said reaching for a hug. *"Where you about to walk to?"* *"On the hill side to Diamonds..."* *"No your not"*, she said getting up to grab her car keys, *"let me grab a jacket"*. When they got out in front of Diamond's house and Quincey was getting out of the car, Cindy said, *"You better make sure you call me when you get ready to leave, you hear me?"* *"Yes"*. *"I love you"*. *"I love you too"*. Diamond was already at the door when Quincey stepped foot on the front porch. *"Hi baby"*. *"Hey sweetheart"*. *"Come on"*, she grabbed his hand pulling him in the house. *"Did you eat baby?"* *"Yeah, my Aunt Cindy forced me to eat some liver and rice"*. *"What you mean forced you?"* *"I never ate it, even when my mom makes it. It was good doe, I ate two plates of that"*. *"Well come on in here and let me give you a massage"*. *"What's up with the robe?"* *"Just got out of the shower baby, look, I don't have anything on yet"*, she said flashing him. They went up to her room and she had him strip down to underwear and socks and lay across the bed while she gave him a full body massage. *"You like that baby?"* *"Mmm..., I do, but I want you to feel special today, come here"*, he whispered as he flipped over and sat up. He untied her robe and gently caressed both of her breast rolling the nipples ever so softly in between his thumbs and fingers. Then he started to trace circular motions around the surface of the nipples causing a tingle through Diamond's body. He rolled her on to the bed kissing her forehead, then her eyelids, the tip of her nose, ears, neck, and then he slid his tongue in her mouth and French kissed her. He was ravishing her body and she was loving it. He moved on sucking on her nipples planting soft wet kisses on her breast. She would purr in between short breaths like a kitten caressing his back. *"Yes baby...take me I'm yours"*. He ran his tongue all over her stomach, then fell in love with her navel sliding down to her hips planting soft kisses there, *"You like that?"* *"I...ooh...love it baby"*. He traced the small strip of pubic hair that barely covered her pelvic area. She arched her back and then he dove in sucking her clitoris swirling his tongue causing her to lose her mind, when she clutched the sheets, he entered her. She made a sound as if she had just dove in a pool of ice. *"Fuck me daddy. Ooooh...ooh baby, harder...fuck...me!"* He was penetrating her long and hard, *"I'm cum...ming...ooh...yes. Shit!"* At that time, Quincey done reached his peak. *"I'm about to bust...ah".* *"Fill this pussy baby, cum wit me"*, she begged him. *"I love you Quincey"*. But she never told him she missed her period cause she wanted to wait until his birthday to give him the news. *"Lay down"*, she ordered. She re-enacted the same treatment that he gave her, then she lifted his dick and sucked in the scrotum and sucked them really gently spitting the testicles out one at a time. Diamond kept running her tongue up and down. When she saw him grab hold of the sheets, she knew she touched a nerve and attacked that area. *"That's it, right there"*, as he could no longer resist the temptation and grabbed her hair. Diamond's approach was as if she was more turned on by him when Quincey pulled her hair. *"Mmm"*, he let out a slight roar, which encouraged her to enhance her capabilities and pursue her ultimate goal. When he came, that was the only place he needed to be on earth. He kissed her forehead and cradled her head to his chest. *"What, I'm a do with you girl?"* *"Anything you want to daddy"*. *"See, this gonna be the reason you end up pregnant, watch"*. Diamond smiled to herself but said nothing rubbing his chest as she lay there peacefully. After chatting with Diamond for a while, he said, *"Let me call aunt Cindy to come get me before she goes to sleep"*. *"But I don't want you to leave baby, nooo"*, she whined pleading her case. *"Look, let me go home, grab something for school and as soon as everybody sleep, I'll call a cab and come on back"*. *"Don't have me waiting up for nothing if your not coming"*. *"You need to trust me"*, he said poking her nose. When Cindy dropped him off and he got into the house, everybody was together in the front room watching a movie. So he shut the door quietly not wanting to interrupt what they were watching, and tried to tip toe up the steps when his mother paused the movie calling out to him, *"Quincey?" "Boy don't be creeping around here, where you coming from?"*

"I just got dropped off by Aunt Cindy, she took me to see Diamond and picked me up". "Uh huh..." "Forreal , that's..." "I know where you was at, I'm talking bout you and her, you know what I'm talking about, don't try to play me". "Ain't nobody tryna play you mom, you all nosy". "Boy ain't nobody nosy, everybody in this room is my business, so I have a right to know. Ya'll two look cute together". "Anyway, *what ya'll watching?" "Diamond in the rough",* she teased. *"No it ain't". "No baby, it's black and blue. I thought it would be good for them to see since all these cops been getting killed". "You mean some more got killed?"* He acted as if he didn't even know what was going on knowing he was the cause of it. *"Two more this morning, that's why I tell you to make it back home, cause you know until they find who's doing it, everybody black will continue to look alike to them no matter how small, light, dark, or tall". "How far into the movie are ya'll?" "Only about fifteen minutes",* said Robbin. "My little sister knows how to tell time?" Quincey joked. *"Shut up punk".* He joined the family and watched the movie until it went off. *"Alright one and two, ya'll got your stuff laid out for school tomorrow?"* "Yes", they answered in unison. *"If ya'll getting a snack, go ahead".*

Quincey texted Jeff to see if he was still awake. *"Yeah, what's up?" "I got caught up with Diamond and she needs me to stay the night, but I wanted to check on the basement feel me?" "I got you, but yo, be careful out there. If you want, I'll come and get you". "I'm good bruh. I appreciate you anyway".* Quincey checked again to make sure his mother was sleep before he called a cab. He had been waiting for at least a half hour or so and figured it would be hard to get a cab out in the project area due to all of the cop killings that had been previously happening. He called Diamond letting her know the situation and suggested that she was going somewhere else instead, but thought again. *"Just let me know when you get in the cab and I'll just meet you at the A-Plus"*. *"I'm calling now baby"*. Quincey started to write again while he was waiting for Diamond to call him back. He thought deep about what he really wanted to say choosing his words carefully. Just as he got into his writing even more, *"but I'm staying on the phone wit you, kay?"* Quincey quietly left out the back door inserting his key to place the top lock back in place so his mother wouldn't suspect that he had been out. He decided to walk in the shadows to prevent being seen by any cops looking forward to creating a hostile environment for anyone being black, including chicken. When he got near the Laundromat he could see the cab was already there parked in front of the store. *"I'm crossing the street now"*.

Just as the cab was pulling out into traffic, several police cars came from out of nowhere with sirens blaring pulling a vehicle over that looked to be an elderly black couple doing nothing other than going the speed limit. It brought pain to Quincey's mind seeing the disrespect piled on by these government officials that were the wrong definition for the word. When you think of the government, you were supposed to think of people, but these cops weren't people, they were inhuman where heartless and brutal best described them. His mind was continuously working in overtime, *"There is a way even the score, ain't no doubt in my mind"*, he kept his thoughts to his self.

CHAPTER 6

That following morning, he and Jeff met up on the side of the school building like they normally did. *"What's up man?" "You man. What's up with you knowing that you got things to do and you over there building a house?"* *"Nah, I'm trying to get my house and affairs in order so that everything is in its proper place when all things are finally finalized".* *"I can respect that, but you got to be on point man".* *"Trust me. But yeah, about the basement situation, I was thinking about going deep and pulling a page out of the history books. Now if you feel like this is way too much for you, I get it, no hard feelings".* *"Nah"*, Jeff said not knowing what exactly it was that he was about to agree to, *"I'm down for it".* *"Here, watch this so you can see first hand what was being done to the innocent, just to instill fear into the others so that they didn't try to do anything in regards of being rebellious against the slave owners".* When Jeff was finished watching the clips of foul acts performed or carried out by his ancestors, he was embarrassed that he was somehow a distant relative of such savages. *"Damn, we don't ever hear about any of these details from the textbooks in our history class. Damn...this was some bullshit".* Jeff was finally at a loss of words, unable to fathom the truths of his Anglo Saxon heritage. *"Now when you put two and two together, you understand, or rather say, comprehend it for what it really is when you look at the judicial system. They never had all of these police stations, or courthouses, or prisons. This shit was non-existent. Soon as honest Abe give the order to release the slaves, it caused a panic prevalent to all plantation owners fearing that the no longer slaves would now be equal to the whites, but take over nearly all of the jobs knowing that they weren't really skilled in trades by profession. They ate off the backs of the slaves, so once you set them free, the fear is where is the new wealth going to come from. Damn, the economy's crashing, cause these petty mutha fuckas is thinking about their own pockets that they don't see the bigger picture. Now...instead of going to make an honest living, they start to rig and manipulate the system cause the Afrikans don't raise a flag".* "What you mean raise a flag?" Jeff asked. *"In them days, as before those, or in previous history, when you were claiming something such as land, freedom, another country, you planted your flag claiming your stake. Now they done sabotaged everything including the constitution where we said to be three fifths of a human being. Clinton changed it when he served his term in 98. They started the new investment plan..."* "Investment plan?" Quincey asked scratching his head. *"The legal system. They didn't really have harsh laws over here except, for savages they used from the London prisons who were used for the purpose of rape, pillaging, murder, diseases, etc...Once they had the Indians land then they had to figure out what to do with the savages. Now once the Afrikans were freed though, they had came up with the scheme to keep their foot on their neck and still make money off them. The trick no one ever paid close attention to, was what to do with a book."* "Wha...what you mean?" Jeff stuttered. *"Their mission statement from a nigger is to put it in a book".* "Well how you figure?" *"I'm a have to hip you to some history. But they did it cause nines time out of then ten, who was gonna pick up a book and read? You'd be hanged for such crime".* "A crime?" *"That's what they made it like where on God's green earth, would you teach the student to be smarter than the teacher. So reading was outlawed. Most of the Afrikans didn't speak English, and if you did it was very little and only what you were taught which was basically what you can and can't do".* All Jeff could say was, "Damn". *"There go the bell right there. Look, I'll probably wait out here for you after school, and then we can finish talking about what I put together for dude in the basement". "Alright",* Jeff gave Quincey a pound, they walked in together and then broke off going their own separate way. Soon as class was let out, Quincey stood on the side where he said he would be waiting for Jeff. Soon as he saw Jeff, he hopped off the ledge, *"What up bruh?" "Man, I couldn't wait to get out of that class". "What happened in there?" "That girl I was telling you about keep on passing me notes after I told her I'm good. She might of passed me a whole notebook worth of notes, she's alright, but she act a little thirsty". "She might be trying to catch me before somebody else step on her feet".* Quincey laughed, slapped Jeff on the back and said, *"Sometimes you need to really pay attention to what's in front of you, cause you end up finding yourself in a situation that you didn't really need to be in especially those crazy ones". "Yeah...I hear you, but that's why I choose to be single, that way I ain't got to deal with the crazy broads. I'm under thirty, how many dudes you know that can defeat temptation?" "Temptation do got a mean record, and you finally made a point that's valid". "Yeah alright". "Where do you wanna go and talk?"* Quincey only asked so they could get away from other eyes and ears when Jeff stalker popped up. *"Jeff, Jeff, can I give you a ride, my mother is right over there?"* The girl said pointing in the direction of a white convertible Mercedes Benz. *"Look Savannah, I appreciate the offer, but me and my friend were talking about something very important and I would appreciate it if I could probably take you up on that offer some other time or something cause I got to really take care of this". "Okay Jeff, but if you ever need a ride, I got you, okay?" "Thank you Savannah". "Yo, she nice, what wasn't to like about that, and she got a nice name. Savannah". "I ain't say nothing about she wasn't, I'm saying if bottom line is, she likes me, then let nature take on its own course. Who wants to be in a relationship where only one party likes the other. I don't need a trophy to sport". "No doubt, I feel you. But listen, I was offered to go back and do another sit down, with that morning show click on CBS, so I think I'm a take her up on her offer so the world have a realistic understanding". "So how long you think that might be to get on?"*

*"I believe I can convince her within the next two days, maybe tomorrow". "Man,
you ain't getting on there by tomorrow". "Bet",* Quincey said extending his hand
for Jeff to shake. They shook hands on it, and then they finished speaking
about the future events with Benjamin and went their separate ways. Soon
as Quincey got home he raced up the steps to his room and threw his book
bag on the bed and started texting his Aunt Cindy. She texted him back
giving him the reporter for the patriot one newspaper phone number. He
dialed the number and waited for an answer. *"Yeah, hello?...This is Quincey
Whitaker, I am the best friend...I was trying to sit down with you and also get in
touch with the lady from*

CBS...yes...okay, thank you." Within the next twenty minutes, Quincey
received a call from Kathuran McNeal explaining that she would love to
have him featured on the show tomorrow, but the only problem was he need
an adult to accompany him.

Quincey didn't want his mother to question him about anything he felt
he would have to explain, so instead, he decided to ask his aunt being as
though the subject was more so about her late son then it was about anything
else. Quincey dedicated his spare time to prepping himself for tomorrow. He
decided to walk over to his aunt Cindy's house, that way it would be hard
for her to turn him down face to face. She opened the door in the same spirits
as always when she saw that it was him. *"Hi baby". "What's up aunt Cindy?"
"Just sitting here looking over some paperwork, nothing important why?" "Well
I...you remember when that Ms. McNeal lady offered us back on her morning show".
"Yeah". "That's why I called for the number I had asked you for. I was...we'll we
was offered on the show tomorrow if you are willing to go with me..." "Boy you think
you so slick". "What?"* He couldn't help himself, and let out a short laugh.

"You would of asked me when you called the first time for the reporters number, you need an adult don't you?" "Yes". *"And you was afraid to ask your mom?"* "No, I didn't feel like being hassled about why I wanted to go, and all that". *"Took the short cut, huh?"* *"Something like that".* *"Well what time you got to be down there?"* *"About 7:15 a.m. or 7:30 a.m., I don't need all that extra stuff, like makeup and all of that".* *"Alright, I normally be up a 6 a.m. anyway, so you can either come over, or just meet me at my car".* They sat and chatted for quite some time before Quincey decided to go home and get ready. When he got home, he gave a little of his time to his family, then he called Diamond, Jeff, and a few other people before he turned in for the night.

Come 5 a.m. Quincey was already wide awake pacing back and forth coaching his self for the manner in which he would conduct himself knowing it would be a touchy subject. He had already showered and dressed, so all he had to do, was walk out the door. After he ate breakfast and spoke to his mother about a few things, he hugged, kissed her on the cheek, did the same to his brother and sister and left out the door and headed straight to his Aunt Cindy's house. When he got in the door, Cindy was already up sipping hot tea watching the news. *"Good morning nephew".* *"Oh, my bad, I was in my head trying to make something come together without people being offended. You know, just like music, everybody be mainly saying the same thing, but the way they formulate it is what really attacks the crowd?"* *"Delivery?"* *"Right".* *"Well, right here"*, Cindy patted her chest and said, *"That's how your point gets delivered. You speak from right here. Come on, cause it's about that time anyway".* They got to the studio a bit early and just basically roamed around seeing how everything worked, and then it was time. *"Right this way ma'am, sir"*, one of the director's said escorting the two of them on the set. After shaking everybody's hand, Kathuran signaled for the camera crew to start filming.

"Hi, and Good Morning America. I have here with me this morning, for the second time, Ms. Cindy Williams, the mother of deceased Trevon Williams, who was a victim of gun violence by a police officer. And here also to the right of me is the cousin, and best friend who gave us a lot of food for thought his last visit here on the show. Now, I wanna get right down to it so that no time is wasted. Ms. Williams, I know you had to see the news lately with all of those indictments, with one of them being the officer involved in your son's death. What was going through your mind at the time of seeing it?"

"Ms. McNeal, I'm not a revengeful type of person, and I always believe life will deal with individuals on its own terms, and time". "Yes, that shows a lot of humanity". "Well I'm only here to support my nephew, he has a lot that he wants to share". "Okay. Then, let me focus on Mr. Whitaker. There has been a string of unsolved cop killings right here in the city, what do you say to that?" "I think that I speak for whoever is responsible for the killings when I say…you took out more than you've put in, and now it's time to be held accountable, something that I've yet to see, is a officer in the wrong, acknowledge that he is, or she is wrong and take full responsibility in doing so. Every time that a situation like this occurs, they always put a black guy, whose thinking about nothing other than a check, up there behind a podium to take the heat off of these white cops. He knows nothing makes sense, but says it anyway. That's boot licking 101". Kathuran was about to ask a question, saw that Quincey was getting ready to speak again and said, "No, excuse me, please continue". "A lot of white people in this country doesn't know any real history, so they think that we are ungrateful to be apart of this country that was snatched from the Indians who were the second people to build this nation and everything in it. Those that inherited wealth, is basically eating off the backs of the slaves. I mean look at the new America, and who are they?" "That's a very good question that I don't have an answer for". Kathuran continued to show interest. "A *monumental of whites lie from day one, even being the reason people of other races believe that we have no place in this world. Take for example the Irish, they were the first slaves of this country who had the nerve to look down on us once they were rejected for poor work and given the job as overseer. Then you look at the Italian who act as if they can't stand blacks, but even as they are married, their mistress is always black. They tell their children these false stories of King Hannibal, who was a African king who conquered Italy, so they painted in their story telling about him being a rapist and other crap, because they were embarrassed to be dominated by his ability to rule. What female would to be married to somebody who watched one man kill 72,000 people, that he probably knew?"* Everybody started to laugh, at Quincey's last remark. *"You got a point there. And now...Mr. Whitaker, what do you think could have been done to fix this type of situation?" "Well you can't really fix anything of this magnitude, but you do the best of you can to try and prevent it from happening again. For example, no one is ever fired, they do everything in their power to protect their pension. Look at the cops in New Jersey almost ten years ago, got caught planting drugs on minorities. For thirty or more people, they handed out 2.5 million dollars, which is a slap in the face after most of them did serious time before the cops were caught. They didn't fire any of them, they were transferred to different boroughs, and the chief spoke highly of the officers stating that they all deserved metals, and said that they were getting criminals off the street by doing what they had to do. The kick is, these people that show their enmity for black people, they don't hide what they feel, but it'll never work in your favor in a courtroom. Look at Trump, he's supposed to be our president. Talking about he wanted to do away with people suing for false imprisonment whether they did one year, or a hundred. In his mind, he already knew who the leading race was to go to jail for false allegations. My father is one of them who just got a new trial. Knowing he's innocent, they will still take him through the same process that landed him there, which is a flawed justice system that targets the minority for monetary gain". "My, young man, you possess a ton of knowledge. Why do you believe, in your own words, that nothing will ever be done about the killings?" "Correction, something is being done, it just took some time. Welcome to today and not yesterday". "And what exactly do you mean?" "One generation prepares for the next. Those that come before me spent a lot of time talking, making slow progress while the whites always tried to talk us down from being violent, that was yesterday".* Cindy was looking at Quincey kind of strange, amazed at how eloquent he was in the language that he spoke, but also to her, he seemed very mature for his age, and wise beyond his years, *"And...Mr. Whitaker, what do you say to your peers who become scared when they see police, or have run ins with them, what do you say to them? Look directly in that camera, over there and tell your peers what exactly it is that you want them to know". "Everything that I do is for every last one of you. But I want you to promise yourselves that you would never let a blind, or a deaf person lead you anywhere. Those who never look where they dwell will never be able to get over the obstacles that life throws at you, and those who are mute, refusing to say anything out of fear is much worse than the ones pulling the trigger. We will all eventually die in the end, but how do you wanna be remembered in your time dying, lies the question. You have to go through the times of difficulty. It is not a one man show. In these coming days you will have to be each other's eyes and ears, times will toughen, but you have to be each other eyes and ears, times will toughen, but you have to make it work, but I promise you that I will bring us victory".* Kathuran didn't necessarily understand what exactly Quincey was talking about, but she wanted to throw both of her hands up and cheer him on. *"We've been humiliated, we've been tortured, disrespected, you name it. No one should live like that and it sets a bad example for your children, and your children's children. Be somebody other than a stepping stool. When you get your opportunities, run for every office possible. Move out the old, and move in the new, it's the only way you will see a positive change."*

"All of these singer rappers who ya'll make rich, if they aren't trying to get into these seats, offices, or white house, then stop supporting them. You do realize that when you buy that garbage, that money never returns to the community and the ones who oppress you invest that wealth back into their communities". "That's impressive. I admire you in all honesty young man, I've learned a lot. Yeah, well in the last month or so, I learned a lot. It's called research. No one really likes to take the time and do research. All of this technology we have at our fingertips, and we waste the time on playing games and social media. Researching your history to find out who you really are, is a beautiful thing. And please, this isn't a time where you go out looking for trouble. Don't throw rocks unless you've been stoned first, and then that's when you send a message to be heard. Only in the beginning, was it peace without war".

"Mr. Whitaker, why do you think not all, but some police officers have such a negative perception of African Americans, if you will?" "Well you know, as a child, or baby rather, you do things out of instinct, but as you grow, most things are taught to you, or you pick them up out of habit. For example, Martin Luther King's best friend when he was little was white. The young white male didn't understand what it was like to hate the opposite race, until his father taught him. So you see, my best friend today is white, even with all that surrounds us, because my parents never showed any of those characteristics, or attempted to force fee hate in the home. My Aunt Cindy", he said pointing to her, "One of the best examples if you ever needed one. Even as that cop did what he did, she could not find it in herself to hate him regardless of how angry and upset she was. But they learn it in the homes, and trying to fit in with people they find to be cool. For the most part, it's a hatred created from

fear that the Afrikans will return to his and her rightful place, which is on the throne. And what that does Ms. McNeal, is create the fear causing chaos and pandemonium amongst the European race who believe they will be stripped away from wealth and white privilege. You remember the Lincoln assassination that was taught in school? It was missing most of the story. Key example. When Lincoln said that slavery has to be abolished, and that he basically had no choice, people thought that he was showing compassion for the negroes, never forget that Lincoln owned quite a bit of slaves, but his strategy was to save the economy, but other whites took it as a indication that, if I lose my slaves that I paid for, I lose my wealth cause I'm not qualified to do any of these jobs that requires labor, and if the slave is equal to me, not only will white privilege be stripped away from me, but where will I find work. That's the fear even of today. What if everything was in reverse, you see how European s commit suicide when they lose a job paying over a hundred grand a year feeling like they can't provide for their families pulling off an insurance scam?" Let *that sink in for those who never heard black people speak without watering down their dialect". "But now, cause we're running out of time, but before we go, and as the last time, it's a joy to have you. I want you to know that I share your pain, and it is ubiquitous, (existing everywhere at the same time), and no one really has a legitimate reason for acting out in these manners, and I say,* she looked into the camera, *"stop killing people, but mostly, you're killing babies". "I'll leave you with this because you just made my point in this game of chess. It has been the strategy of white racist men for years, that if you kill off the seeds (children), how can you have an existing future?" "Although that being said, I am your host Kathuran McNeal, right here on your morning show on CBS 21. Until next time".*

"Boy you something else", Cindy whispered tapping Quincey on the leg. They both got up shaking hands with Kathuran, and the production crew hands. When they made their exit, Stacy was waiting just out front talking on her cell phone when she acknowledged them holding up one finger with a smile to go along with it. Cindy frowned at Quincey, then asked, *"Boy, what you getting me into, your mom know about this?" "I'm cool from here, I'm not getting you into anything, promise. I'm about to do a interview with her to print an article, that's all". "You better be". "I'll call you soon as I leave here". "Alright, give me a hug, and make sure you call me". "I will. I love you Aunt Cindy". "I love you to".* Cindy had a ill feeling that something was about to occur, sort of like the day her son died. When she got in her car, she immediately texted Karmen a message letting her know to call her as soon as possible concerning Quincey.

CHAPTER 7

Stacy wrapped up her phone conversation and walked to the driver side of her car signaling for Quincey to get in. "Have you eaten already?" "Yeah, I ate", "Well I need to eat something, my stomach is empty honey. I'll just go to Jimmy the Hot Dog King, or whatever he call it, since we already near that way". "No problem". When they entered the diner and seated themselves Stacy placed her order. "You sure you don't want anything?" "I'll just have an orange juice, no ice please". "So what brings us together this morning?" Stacy asked out of curiosity, because it wasn't the norm for a high school student and a journalist to be meeting up with each other on a school day. "I would rather have some privacy, but do believe that it's very important. But what you have that I don't have, is a long reach in the media world, far more advanced than just Facebook, or Instagram. You print news". "Okay". Stacy thought to add on something else but stopped in mid-sentence as her plate was being placed in front of her. "We need to be a team for what needs to be done for our people, but if we are going to work together with your approval, of course, but I need you to give me your word after I give you information which I am sure should persuade you in the right direction". "Well I'm need a bit more than that baby, cause the mere thought of you peeing on me and trying to convince me that the taste on my tongue is just hot rain, is a bit deeper than words honey". Quincey smirked at the quick response figuring that one response deserves another. "I'm not out to game you", he said through a chuckle, "my intentions are..." "Don't you forget, I grew up in them same projects, don't be fooled by the other education". She interrupted giving a verbal warning. "Look, this isn't one of them relationships where I got you by telling you what you wanna hear, not in my blood. I just want to make sure there are no regrets in the end". "Regrets about what?" She stopped eating, staring at Quincey awaiting a response. "Please, enjoy your food, finish up, we'll talk".

Stacy rushed her meal curious as to what he had to say that was actually worth her time this morning. She had already hung up on some important information back in front of CBS Studio in order to hear what Quincey had to say, so she crossed her fingers walking out the door hoping he had some valuable information that would make headlines, "Anywhere you want to go in particular?" "Just anywhere wit no extra set of ears". "Let's walk the river-front since it's right there, that way we'll be by ourselves". "No doubt". They finally found a place to park and began walking. "So what's so important where my help is needed?" "Let's say hypothetically..." "Boy, is you serious..." "You got to hear me out in order to see where I'm going with this. Now, hypothetically, I know the person whose been killing these cops. And soon, he wants to turn himself in, but, he wants to apologize personally to the whole police department, but, he do not want any reporters to show up in fear the police may not want to talk, or bring him in, alive once he explains why he did it. But most importantly, he wants to mail you and Ms. McNeal a video for one to air, and one to print explaining to the world why they committed these acts..." "I thought you said a person, so it's more..." "Nah, just one. But what's really needed of you, is your word. I have a video in a safe location, already ready to be delivered to you, and Ms. McNeal, but, your main task, is trying to keep other reporters away from the area that person chooses to be arrested". "What you mean, how am I going to keep thirsty reporters away from somewhere?" "I can give you a little bit of help with that. After you and Ms. McNeal finish your stories, then you guarantee everybody their own copy, delivery after that person is taken in". "What makes you trust me?" "I don't, that's why I sleep alone". "Boy you too much". "Also, that's why I didn't give a name, everything leads to a dead end anyway". "So what now?" "You do your part, but you will get the video the day after". "Why the day after, I can get the story from whatever location myself?" "First of all, you won't get the full story, and secondly, you may not get to print a story if the situation turn bad. They don't care who they shoot around here, it's at your own risk just like in those countries, not worth risking your life for something you may never see", he wagged his finger at her shaking his head, then went on to say, "God forbid, you don't make it back, then what?" "Ain't no God forbid, that's on them, I'll do what I can, but I ain't making no promises, you can't keep an ignorant ass person away from a good story". "Well, if something do go wrong, God bless". "Why you say it like that?" "We not talking about a white person, they do everything in their power to bring them in alive even in stand offs. That's how you know they be lying when they be talking bout how quick they can close in on you from twenty feet, that somebody welding a knife. But them white boys be busting AK's, AR's, anything heavy at the police, and in the mist of gun fire, they still trying to talk'em down". "Just come on son, put the gun down", "if you black", "their all dangerous, I had to neutralize him". "You ain't never lied, they did that in that McDonald case, he wasn't nowhere near'em, then they lied on the report, and held the tape for about two years". "I always wondered what black people was thinking to actually want to survive the boat ride to America, but then, once you got here, to allow you and your children to work in the fields, they would have been sent me back on the boat going for the next pick up, I promise you". "Boy you crazy". "Nah, I'm just real. They would have had a easier time getting the labor out of their parent and kids before I would of stepped foot in the middle of a field. You seen the OG on the remake of Roots", she said, when they call us up to entertain them, we jump over and take our chances with the sharks, but one way or the other, she was out of there. Whatever stories they told about fu bob, she wasn't bout to find out, now was she". "I feel you, but listen, if I'm a do my part, I got to be making some calls, so that means I need to be heading back to the office". "I'm about to go holla at my peoples soon as you drop me off".

"That story should put you in a good position, I promise you, you can even sell it and come up, cause it's gonna be top fire". Stacy stopped near a curb to let Quincey out, he thanked her, looked back and said, "I got you. As I swore to keep it one hundred, make sure your promise remains the same". She nodded her head, waved, and drove off beeping the horn. Quincey had sent a text to Jeff making sure that everything was still in place for midnight tomorrow. When he didn't receive the response he was looking for, he sent another text back informing Jeff that he would meet up with him later. He then went home to mail off the letters that he wrote to make sure he didn't forget to mail them out. He went in quickly, retrieved the letters, and exit making his way to the mailbox. He then made his way to the stash spot to retrieve the gym bag he had packed in preparation for his visit to see Benjamin. He locked the van door back, and proceeded in route to his destination. Soon as he entered the back door, he kept hearing a muffled sound coming from down in the basement. He unlocked the latch, walked down the steps and protruded the bag around the banister just in case Benjamin had somehow gotten loose and tried to ambush him. When Quincey peered around the banister, he started laughing when he realized that the muffled sounds was Benjamin crying for help if anyone took the time to rescue him. Quincey dropped the bag and stared at Benjamin long and hard with a quizzical look on his face. He walked over and peered at Benjamin before he removed the tape around his mouth. When he aggressively unwrapped the tape, he asked, "Why did you pull the trigger, it's just me and you here?" "Benjamin just looked up as if confused, and said nothing. Quincey reached for the razor and cut the tape to allow Benjamin to free his arms. He went in the bag and pulled out a bag from Hardee's and threw it to Benjamin who didn't bother to catch it. "Go head", Quincey said pointing to the bag as if it was a obvious guess what it was. Benjamin slowly reached for the bag checking the contents inside examining them closely before eating. "If I wanted you dead, you'd be there already".

Benjamin greedily gobbled the food in the bag, Quincey tossed a bottled water to him and said, "Take ya time, no rush". After guzzling half of the bottle, Quincey said, "You answer me as to why I'm still alive, and I'll answer any questions you got for me". "My goal, is to get you in front of the camera, and tell the whole world why you pulled that trigger". "Hell, that's just who tf I am, ol' country boy taught to hate niggers. Heck, in the world we live in, white...,is always right. I mean, it's too late for me to change...hell...I done killed a lot of niggers in my time and slept peaceful at night, and see, that's the difference between you and I, you don't have that fire in ya belly. See this here", he said pointing to the tape around his legs, "If the shoe was on the other foot, you be dead right now". "Is that right, and I believe that's why the shoe is on the right foot. See, the real difference that separates me from you", he said pointing at Benjamin, "is you don't have no real legitimate reason as to why you done what you did, I do 'Ignoramus' has no time to prepare for any event where there is aftermath because they lack knowledge to prepare one's self. That's another one wrong for the white folks. You boys and girls are really scraped deep down inside, I know what you fear. Fate would never allow you to annihilate my peoples. God's punishment to my peoples really have nothing to do with yours". "What are you talking about, this is a race war between black and white". "Do ya'll white folks even know how to fight, I believe America's independence was hand delivered by the 5,000 slaves that fought on that front line. There is no race war yet, only reason most of you stupid ass crackas is still alive. What you think slavery just happened cause of smart people like you. Ha! Your belief system is very disappointing, but tell me this since you got it all figured out, how would anybody exist on this planet without us?" "Boy you confused, it was us first, why you think Hitler was killing all those Jews, they were God's chosen people, none of them had nappy hair and dark features or skin..." "You Europeans faked yourselves out stealing other peoples history", Quincey said cutting him off, "There was no Europeans living in Egypt, Israel, or anywhere else where over a hundred degrees a melt something". "You do realize that European Jews came at a later time through the scattering of people and race mixing, cause Yiddish is a language derived from medieval High German, written in the Hebrew alphabet and spoken by East European

Jews. Hebraic is the original language of the Hebrews who became the Israelites, which is a ancient Semitic language the Afrikans spoke. See, if you Europeans stop tampering with everybody's history, the story of truth wouldn't be hidden from yourself. Now ya'll done gave these Europeans a home, and reparation for some shit that ain't have nothing to do with Christ. Ya'll done made up a name that's of Greek origin, hung pictures of a blonde hair, blue eyed faggot in the churches, killing slaves who spoke of the true Christ Huron. How obsessed can you people be with yourselves you's a bitch without ya gun. If ya'll didn't have guns, then what?" "Challenging me I see. Really tryna' get free huh? I tell you what, if you beat me in a fair one". "What's a fair one?" "A one-on-one, fist fight, just me and you, nobody's here but us. I won't even try and track you down, my word". "Boy you bullshittin' me", Benjamin let out a loud cackle as if he was intoxicated. "No strings attached, I know what you thinking, I like my chances". Quincey cut the rest of the tape, allowing Benjamin time to stretch but watching him with a keen eye making sure he didn't try anything funny. "I guess you get to live out your TV fantasy".

Soon as Benjamin got up off the floor and squared off Quincey pulled a taser from behind his back and pulled the trigger hitting Benjamin in the center of his chest. "Get ya dumb ass back in the corner dickhead". "I thought you was giving me your word?" "I did, I gave you a chance, what you do wit it when you get it is on you". Quincey squeezed the trigger again, and again. "You didn't give Trevon a fair one, did you?" He was a bit too disorient to say anything so Quincey squeezed the trigger one more time, and before you knew it, he was taping up Benjamin's legs, turned him back over, punched him in the face leaving him in an incapacitated state, sitting him up taping his arms to his sides. Quincey decided to leave the gym bag in the basement being as though he had to make another trip back there anyway. He left out securing the locks and started making his way over to meet Jermy. On his way to the park, he came across a basketball which was handy for the task ahead. He saw a weird lanky white guy up ahead, gave it a blank thought feeling sure that was Jeff. He finally made it to the flat top and passed the ball to Jeff who took a shot. "That's a pretty nice stroke big fella". "Should of saw me when I actually played, all state, played a year of college at Colgate before I blew a knee". They shot around while Quincey was explaining what exactly it was he wanted done. "I know we went over it already, I just want it to be precise. You can never be ready enough". "You got a nice shot there yourself". "I play for the high". "Lot of good talent come out of John Harris, but nobody really seems to do anything with it". "Yeah, you right about that. I mean, I guess it got to be your dream, something you're passionate about. The ones who were passionate, weren't really that good". "Yeah, you got a good point. AH...who knows". "Anyway, on both sides, the streets aren't that wide, a lot of cars is going to get the wrong end of the stick". "For a good cause right?" Jeff took another shot and waved Quincey to tag along to show him what he started so he had better insight. "And see, normally when an emergency call goes out, every car will line up on both of these streets, and the even smaller ones on the right and left. Everything is already laid down, you can't even tell, look just like the street. Also got some of those things you asked about for the vehicles, only somewhere around ten or twelve of'em". "That'll help, especially for the message I'm trying to get out there". "Absolutely, get you started in the right direction, now let me show you how to work the masterpiece that controls it all". As he was showing Quincey how to work the control, he asked about the podium he requested with bulletproof glass that would project him in case of a minor interruption. "That's what I'm talkin' bout right there my boy, give me some". After he dapped Quincey up, Quincey face timed Jeff to make sure he was home so he could pick him up. "I need you to meet me over everything one more time while they waited for Jeff to pull up". By the time Jeff finally parked and got out, Jeff and Quincey were back on the topic of basketball. Jeff tapped on the window to get their attention alarming the two of them. Soon as Quincey saw that it was Jeff and was immediately relieved, glad that it wasn't a police officer instead. He jumped out walking all the way to the back of Jeff's van and removed first, the podium, and then the other two bags and loaded them in the van that Jeff drove. Quincey got dropped off at home, called his Aunt Cindy as promised, spent some time at home with the family, then went to see Diamond, stayed there until it got dark out said his goodbyes and headed for the streets. Quincey searched every square inch of at least ten blocks looking for a marked unit and saw not one. "Damn, when you don't need'em, they everywhere", Quincey said more so to his self growing more irritated by the minute. He was looking down, so he hadn't yet seen the squad car slowing to a quite creep. He felt somebody watching him so he looked up and noticed the cop holding a pretty long gaze. Quincey kept walking at a snail's pace, and suddenly a beam of light peeked through that little crack in the window he'd been waiting for.

You could see the cop didn't respect the law his self, he parked the squad car, got out with the engine left running, and went into a alleyway nearby where some kids were playing and relieved himself. In that instant, Quincey hurried across the street, eased up on the car, opened the gym bag and placed what looked like a magnet right underneath the wheel base area by the gas tank and slid off. He repeated this identical tactic eleven more times before he called it a night. When he made it home, his mother knew that he had just came in the door because she waited up on him. It had been hard for Karmen to sleep most nights since Quincey's run in with the police near a month ago. "Your plate's on the stove, and where is you coming from this late knowing what done happened to you..." "Mom I'm good..." "Boy you good for the moment, what bout tomorrow, and the day after? These mutha fuckin' cops is killing our babies! You think it's fun not being able to sleep at night, huh? Before Trevon got killed, my hair was all black, look at this", she pulled some of her hair showing Quincey so he could see the few grays she recently inherited from stress. Quincey made his way to the kitchen, washed his hands and grabbed his plate from off the stove. Karmen stormed in the kitchen grabbing Quincey by the chin turning his head towards her, "Boy you better answer me, I can't afford to lose you". Her yelling had awakened the twins, they raced down the steps to see if everything was alright, and instead saw their mother crying on their brother's shoulder while he was holding her. "What's going on?" they asked in unison. "It's alright, ya'll go on back to bed". "Quincey I won't lose you, I won't". "You can never lose me mom, I will always be in the heart, always". They stared that moment for a nice while, and then Quincey encouraged her to go on up stairs to bed. "Don't go back out of this house Quincey". His heart seemed to be hardening ever since the death of Trevon as if his emotions didn't work. He just sat at the kitchen table as if nothing ever happened just eating his meal. After he cleaned the little bit of dishes he used, he went up to his room and cut on the television. When he couldn't find one thing that he wanted to watch, he turned to CNN seeing a panel discussion about the missing police officers, the dead ones, and the one still at large, or either dead. Don Lemon had a pretty decent conversation going, so he tuned in until the second half and cut it off. His mind went totally blank while he was staring at the ceiling with not one thought trapped in solitude. He sprang up, started pacing, mumbling to his self for the next three hours and then he went and took a cold shower. He prepared himself like any other school day, and before he knew it, his mother was calling him down stairs with his siblings to eat breakfast like they normally do. When everyone was out the door. Karmen picked up her phone to check her Facebook page seeing she still had messages that she never checked. When she saw Cindy had left one, she immediately opened it and read it. She pressed the send button and let it ring a few times before she decided to hang up. "I know she's up".

Karmen figured she should just walk over there before both of them went on about their day. Cindy heard the first knock and stuck her head out the window and yelled, "Who is it?" "It's me girl". When she let Karmen in, they greeted each other with a hug and kiss on the cheek. "Girl I'm sorry I hadn't texted you back or called you, I've been on the phone all day yesterday, and when I finished cooking, I took a bath, and went to sleep". "You know Quincey had called for that girl's number who does the newspaper articles, and then he asked me to go to the CBS news show for in the morning we went to. Now at first, I ain't think nothing of it, but then when you hear him speak, you see the maturity but the way he delivers, sends a chill down your spine. It's something I can't really explain, but you know when something ain't right, and you get that strange feeling in the pit of your stomach..." "It's called intuition girl". "I know...shut up, I'm trying to describe the feeling". "He come rolling up in the crib late last night, then he had the nerve to not even hear what I was saying to him. I had to snatch'em up, I ain't playing girl, these boys in blue is out here trippin. Shoot, they almost had him last month". "Yeah, he must of forgot...It's definitely real out here, ain't no question bout that". "Well what you doing later on, you can come on over for dinner, you wanna go to happy hour on your lunch break?" "Yeah...it's been a minute and it ain't like I got anything special to do". "Alright then, where you wanna meet?" "Meet me at the D's, I want some of them wings for lunch".

CHAPTER 8

Quincey sat patiently, waiting for school to let out so he could resume back to carrying out his plans. He talked about nothing much, worried about nothing, and he was humble. He had been very satisfied with his plans, all except the fact that he hadn't been all the way upfront with Jeff about his plans for Benjamin. After he was to help Quincey handcuff him to the gate, he had no knowledge. Afterwards, and he too would find out just like everybody else when he saw streaming live. Quincey sat there daydreaming about all of the things he would never see once it was all over. Still, it was a step in the right direction since Nat Turner, and he felt that the only way to release yourself of the bullying was by punching the bully in the face every time you saw them. When that bell rung, he really jumped up out of his seat to the nearest exit. He waited for Jeff outside the school building, and was surprised to see Jeff walking out the door with Savannah. He sent Jeff a text to let him know that he was going to walk slow so he could talk to Savannah and he didn't get in the way as a third wheel. Jeff finished his conversation, gave Savannah a hug, and ran to catch up to Quincey. "I see you playa". "Nah, nothing like that", Jeff said blushing, "I see you, I noticed the hug, that digit was a bit firm". "GO head man". Jeff pushed Quincey playfully. "Yeah though, I'm a need you on point, we got to go and get dude to clean up and then get'em on over there to Reservoir, so once I get done with the family, then I'll just hit you up. By the way, how's your mom doing?" "She's still so, so, I do the best I can when dealing with her. I'm getting tired of walking around on eggshells". "That's why Savannah's good for you, couldn't of been better timing, and it seems like her mom is cool peoples so you'll be more than likely be able to kick it with her over her spot". Jeff just shrugged it off, "It'll be alright, I just hope she pull it together for herself so it don't effect me in the days coming". "Yeah I hear that". "Just hit me when you ready", Jeff said turning off at the corner so he could be on his way.

Quincey made it in the house, he was bombarded with a ton of questions from his mother. "Why ain't you tell me you went on that show again?" "Aunt Cindy told you?" "Don't worry about who told me, and why didn't you ask me?" "I would have, but I thought I wouldn't of been able to go cause you would have been busy to go and I needed an adult. But she invited me and Aunt Cindy back anyway, so I thought I would just ask her, it wasn't no big deal or anything like that". "Boy what you got going on, too much sneaking around, close encounters with the police, what's next?" Quincey didn't respond. "Boy you better answer me, I know I'm not talking to myself!" "You don't have to worry mom..." "Don't tell me what not to worry about, I'm a mother, that's what I do. Now you got to tighten up baby, cause I ain't cut out to be identifying none of my babies. Sit down", once Quincey was seated, Karmen straightened her posture and looked him directly in the eyes, "I know you have a lot going on up here", she said illustrating tapping her head with the index finger, "We all do, baby you can talk to me, I will listen. We all hurting and the pain don't always go away overnight, but that's what makes us strong as a people, we handle the burden and keep it moving. We are a people of great strength honey, be that great strength, if you can't, I will. I love you Quincey". "I love you too mom", was all he said. He knew his heart would break if he made eye contact, so he looked away, he couldn't allow words to be the reason why he let Trevon die in vain. Karmen knew she was losing him, but how, and why. "I'll be back mom, I'm a go check on

Aunt Cindy real quick". "Quincey, don't be out long". "I'll be right back, promise". "How you knew I was out here?" "Cause your momma called me and told me you was coming". "She's stressing me about being out late..." "Well Quincey I know you see what is going on out there, boy, you was a victim yourself just not that long ago. You are a nigger to them boys in blue, even the ones who don't know they black. Right now it's sudden season, ain't no playing, get caught slippin' if you want. But then again, we the ones who got to worry about that part. Please baby, don't make this hard on your mom". "Everything will be alright in the end". "I don't know what that's supposed to mean boy, but ya scaring me". "You don't need anything done while I'm here?" "Other than for you to listen, nah, I'm good nephew. How about you, you need anything, a ear to listen, a hug, a beating, anything?" "Actually I'm good, I just came to check on my favorite aunt". "Your only aunt". "Indeed, but still my favorite aunt". After about 45 minutes of the two just talking, Quincey finally rose out of his seat, gave Cindy an extended version of his usual hug and headed out the door. "Make sure you give your mom a kiss for me, never mind, I forgot I'm coming over for dinner", "I'll see you then". "Tell her give me a couple minutes, I was caught up in this movie".

When Quincey came back in the house, he asked, "Mom, where the twins at? "Probably upstairs playing that game". Quincey went upstairs to find the twins exactly where his mom said that they might be. He tapped on the door, "Come in". "I should jump on both of ya'll", he said laughing. "I owe you something anyway punk". Robbin snatched the joystick out of Roberts hand and threw it to Quincey and said, "Pick your team". "Hey Karmen". "Girl don't...don't be creeping up on me like that, trying to give me a heart attack". "Alright, that's enough, you ain't got to do all of that. You worser than Fred.

The door was already opened". Cindy wave her hand flagging off Karmen's dramatics and antics. "Why you so late?" Karmen asked looking at her imaginary watch. "Caught up in this movie, you know how I get watching movies. Shoot, if it wasn't for Quincey, I would of still been glued to the tube". "What was you watching?" "It was an older movie called "State of Grace". It's like a mob flick, and some corrupt Irish cops, something like that, you got to watch it. It's good from what I saw so far". "Well let me finish up in here and then we can watch it". "Smells good, what is it?" "Shrimp and linguine. A cheese sauce and a salad". "Anyway, I told Quincey, we are here for him if he needs to talk, vent, whatever, he just seems different. I don't know, could we just be looking too deep into it..." "No, no, I know him, and something up here just clicked", Karmen pointed to her head and snapped her fingers. "You never know til you know, but I'm sure". She finished with the salad, and called the children to come and eat. "Hi Aunt Cindy", the twins spoke in unison. "Ya'll better give me my hugs, what ya'll was doing?" "Me", said Robbin, "I was beating up on Quincey, and him", she said pointing at Robert, "He was holding my jacket while I was breakin 'em off".

They enjoyed a laugh finding it cute that the older brother found the time to play with his younger siblings. After dinner and a movie, Karmen and Cindy ventured off into the kitchen for a night cap and talked for a while. "Well, I kindly thank you for the dinner, the movie, and the conversation with the drink, but I got to run so I can get up on time for work". "Alright then sis, see you tomorrow". They hugged, and then Karmen walked Cindy to the door. She looked in Quincey's direction in an attempt to warn him not to go out, but thought better of it knowing the more you pressure then child, the more they rebel. "Alright ya'll, I'm going on to bed, don't be up too late, and make sure your stuff is laid out for school". After embracing every last one of her children, Karmen went on to retire to her room. Quincey looked at his phone to check the time, and saw that it was 10:45 p.m. He stretched, yawned, then said, "Alright ya'll, I'm out". He hugged the twins a little too long, but they said nothing. He walked in to his room knowing that may be the last time that he see his family let alone, enter his bedroom again. He didn't feel jittery, didn't have butterflies, and out of all the things in the world that he could be, he was calm. He wasn't trying to work his self up while preparing for the task at hand. Other then that, he was humming the song his father suggested he listen to right after losing Trevon. He readied himself to the best of his ability, sent a text to Jeff to make sure he was ready, and laid back on his bed. Twelve o'clock had finally came which was the moment of truth. He checked to make sure his mom was still sound asleep before he made his way out the window. It was already pitch black outside, but Quincey always dressed in all black for the most part, so he was obscured when passing by any cop vehicles, or things of that nature. He scurried along the way trying to hurry as if he had a set time. They made it to their destination without incident, and went straight to the basement and cut on the light. Again, Quincey repeated the same techniques as the last time, and once saw that the way clear or things of that nature. He scurried along the way trying to hurry as if he had a set time. They made it to their destination without incident, and went straight to the basement and cut on the light, again, Quincey repeated the same techniques as the last time, and once saw that the way was clear, he stepped from behind the shadows and appeared before Benjamin who seemed to be sound asleep. He approached Benjamin quietly, and cooked his arm back catching him with a power slap. "Whaaammm!" He smiled at the startled look that finalized in formation across Benjamin's face. "Wake up!" He shouted for no apparent reason at all other than to feel in change, or to have dominion over him as he attempted to do with Trevon that morning that he felt the need to take his life because he wouldn't listen . "This is what's gonna happen. You are going to clean up, eat something, and then ready yourself". "Ready myself for what?" Benjamin had a look of confusion knowing his time was somewhere close to expiring.

"Today, you get to go free. These'll be your last hours spent with us, and then you got two options". "Two options?" "Sure, you can either go to jail after you lose trial on all charges, or you can run. I want the world to see in my home made video, just how easy it is to do the same exact things that you've done to us". When it went over Benjamin's head, Quincey didn't feel the need to evaluate.

After they finished with the cleaning part, Benjamin was wondering why he was putting on a black suit that fit, but the mentioning of him going free changed his argumentative side, and he kept quiet. This time he wasn't taped up as before, they handcuffed him and hauled him off like they done so many black people during his days as a police officer. When they got him in the van by tossing him in, he was tased for what Jeff said was resisting, and then they shackled his feet. Jeff parked across the street from the park and waited for the lights from the park ranger to show so they could track his location. He started the drone up and let it fly soon as he saw the vehicle traveling at a snail's pace of just two miles an hour. Jeff was trying to stall the ranger out waiting for him to stop so the SUV wouldn't roll down hill and hit something such as a tree making a loud noise causing a disturbance in the neighborhood waking people up. He caught his big break when the ranger stopped putting the vehicle in park, killing the engine to drink what looked like a Pepsi soda bottle, with clear liquid. Jeff thought to his self, "It must be alcohol, cause no one takes a break for that, and he just killed the lights". By the time the ranger heard the glass in the back crack, it was too late. He hovered the drone to make sure there was no movement or signaling for help. "Yeah, he dead". He landed the drone and drove up to the flat top of the park.

They carried Benjamin halfway, and then dragged him the rest of the way which wasn't that far, but just so he could see how it felt with the shoe on the other foot. When they got to the gate on the side of the basket-ball court. Quincey said, "That's perfect right there". Jeff climbed to the top of the gate, tied some thick rope around the pole of the fence with the noose part hanging down. Quincey scooped Benjamin like a rag doll, placing his back against the gate pushing his upper body upward, so that Jeff could slip the noose around the neck. Once the noose was in place, Quincey let the bottom half of Benjamin's body drop. He told Jeff to leave him as his gaze held steadfast watching Benjamin's legs that were shackled, thrash around. "I need you to help me get this podium out the van".

Quincey set the podium underneath one of the basketball rims so it would be hard for the cops to have a clear visual of him while he was trying to say what it was that he needed to say. "Listen", he said to Jeff, "I love you man, and I hope it works. Now get on out of here so I can handle my business, and so don't nobody see you. Go straight up and make a right, and go straight down Regina. Make a left at the stop sign, and take Zarker, that way you only have to deal with one light". "I love you to bruh". Jeff gave it some thought the other night that it was a small chance that Quincey was going to come out of this alive, and looking at him now with belts of bullets across his body along with other crazy looking stuff, wasn't no way in the world, he was coming in alive, and the reason why, he was not white. Jeff finally let go, "Alright man, do your thang". Quincey started to call 911, gave his emergency and hung up. He started live streaming explaining why Benjamin was in this predicament. He cut the pants off of Benjamin so that his bottom half was nude, and chopped off his penis, pried Benjamin's mouth open and shoved it in. He looked into the camera on his phone and said, "I am Quincey Whitaker, and I know this isn't the Quincey Whitaker that most of you know. But for those of you who don't know this face. That's officer Benjamin Taggart, the police officer who killed Trevon Williams, my cousin, and best friend right in front of me on our way to school. He ain't even try to conceal the fact that he was going to just throw down a gun as if Trevon was armed trying to reach. Say what now? Uh huh, officer Taggart can't speak. See that, officer Taggart has a full mouth. For those of you who lack knowledge, Willie Lynch is the European responsible for, "breaking a slave", and what they would do, is rape the women, children, hang the men in front of them after making him watch his family being violated, then they would make the family along with other slaves watch them hand the men just like you see ol' officer Taggart here, sept from a tree. This is new and advanced. But you see, they would then cut off the genital or penis if you will, and place that in the mouth. I've done already gave you an example. But you can't sympathize for him because there was no one to sympathize for the slaves. No one wept for them, no one!" He could hear the sirens nearing so he grabbed his mega phone and the lighter fluid. "See this here?" He drenched Benjamin's lifeless body with the lighter fluid making a trail by his foot, and lit a match dropping it. "Then they would do this here", he would demonstrate as if it was a cooking show. "Set that man on fire like that, just to scare the other slaves so that they wouldn't run, or rebel".

Benjamin's body caught a flame, but he didn't think that was enough, so he doused his body with some more. "Uh huh, that's it right there". When he saw the officer exiting their vehicles with guns drawn, he yelled in the mega phone. "I'm not playing a game! All I want is to finish my story and then I will let you take me peacefully. You get ya stupid ass the fuck back over there!

I...AM...DECORATED...WITH...HEAVY...EXPLOSIVES.   Everything around you is on a timer just in case I don't get to finish my story. Also, somebody is watching from a distance just in case you try and take me out, then everybody around you just signed their death certificate because of the stupid mutha fucka who didn't listen! Don't try to be a hero! The only person dead, is him", he said pointing to the dulling flames, "I was explaining the reason why before I was rudely interrupted". He stepped behind the podium to play it safe. "Get me whoever is in charge". "I am". A dark brown skinned man stepped out in the open pointing to himself. "This is why we can never get anywhere as a people, because of crabs just like you". "Listen young brother, I'm just trying to help..." "Shut the fuck up, see, I was gonna give you a shot, cause no one really gives the brother man a shot. But you, you's another nigger, being the puppet and spokesperson for these crackas who keep on killing your own kind! How the fuck is you gone save the day?" Quincey memorized all of the cars that he put the magnet like devices on. "Listen up, if I call your squad car number, raise your hand. "49" An officer raised his hand, Quincey lucked up because that car wasn't boxed in. "You in charge, what's ya name?" "Chief Jennings" "Alright Chief, I don't believe you are really here to help, so I'm a need you to go sit in car number 49 until my story is complete".

Chief Jennings went to sit in the front seat, and Quincey said, "Nah, enjoy the back seat like how the black folk ride, see it from their point of view". Soon as the chief got in the backseat, Quincey said, "Make sure that door's secure, cause he ain't listen". Quincey heard the helicopter above, and said, "see, this is the problem with people who can't listen!" *Boom!* He passed a button causing squad car 49 to explode and disseminate in midair. "I'm really trying here, but ya'll making me out to be the bad guy, who in charge now, cause we ain't using no house niggers, that's why chief had to go, who?" Quincey was pointing in the crowd of cops. "Who are you?" "I'm Lieu...Lieu...Lieutenant..." "A Lieutenant, we got a Lieutenant...that's good. Now, let your people know, I don't wanna hurt anybody, I just wanna tell my story, can I do that please, I won't take too much of your time cause I know ya'll got a lot of important stuff to do, like arrest niggers". "Sure go...go head". The Lieutenant commanded everybody to stand down and lower their guns. "Finish your story young man". That was the Lieutenant's first time speaking without stuttering. "Where was I at, ahem, ahem". He cleared his throat. "Again ol' Benjamin is right here, and the police force is right there because the Europeans who is always stealing the identities of other races, the now Americans who are no longer Indians, but these Europeans, the thieves fail to do right by the people who they labeled niggers in the first place. But what you people who have not a clue need to know this, my people didn't request to be here, they didn't ask for a green card. They were kidnapped by their own people, and traded off for goods the Europeans who delivered us on ships and auctioned us off to the highest bidder. We built this mutha fucking country for what is today, and we spend the most money in this country. We spend at least over 2 trillion dollars a year just shopping!

Then you gone act like you don't need us no more and swap us out with the Mexicans who are in search of a better life, but will work for less. Your constitution is a slap in our mutha fucking face to tell us we're only three fifth of a human being, calling us aliens but continue to tax us and lock us up as if we belong here. This slavery evolution is an act of God, if you know your history, but your time is up. Each man that has come before me, has set the standards that shall be for the new generations. If you are like me, then you are nobody's slave, mentally or physically. Truth is, we allow them to treat us like this cause we refuse to fight in fear of the repercussions. But if you are dead, how do you know. If death is the final stage of the end result, why would you be afraid to take that trip where everybody on the planet eventually goes? For years we prayed for death to claim those that are suffering, are we not a part of those suffering? See boys and girls tuned in to this at home, I am going to lead us to victory today!" Quincey became animated, "These officers here today, have vowed to never kill another black person and try and clean it up as a justifiable homicide. I am going to hold them accountable, right here, on this very day. You mutha fuckas are beyond unbelievable, we picked cotton for ya'll fucking asses, tobacco, corn, all that. The women even breast fed your kids, cooked, cleaned, fed those ungrateful sons of bitches. I'm staring at the product of'em now, the ol' paddy rollers. Then you gone send a house nigger to try and clean this shit up! This ain't spilt milk. You gave these fake ass imposters, who Hitler was killing, a home and reparations cause they was pretending to be original Jews, and he thought they killed his Jesus, another faking his originality. Where is the reparations for the original Jews huh, where is our checks at, you put as through it all, holocaust at ten times the equivalent of theirs, and still putting us through the ringer. For over four hundred years, we still hanging from them same trees cause niggers refuse to do something, but see, this nigger here was a smart one, I did the research. While ya'll letting all ya'll time be consumed with the PlayStations, FaceBook, TikTok, and all of that, I was finding out who I'm supposed to be. My parents raised me to do entertainment right, I was their promise child, but then you", he pointed his finger at the cops, "turned me into this", he pointed to himself. "You people are some of the most fucked up people on the face of the earth, you could be filthy rich, and will let your own mother die just to put one more dollar in your bank account. You've been killing people for oil, you throw your trash in the ocean bringing death to the fish, you got the turtles suffocating from eating plastic bags. This...is...how...history, always repeats itself, by destruction. What you have been building all these years will be the result of a race war because you were never careful. And innocent people will die. The sad part about it is, at least seventy percent of whites was riding for us during the civil rights movement, that was more than our own people, today, it's even more, now just imagine how many will die because of your kind? I don't know why other countries respect America, the only thing they respect is your money, and guns. Other than that, ya'll pussy! Quincey was paying attention to the fore truck, helicopters, and then he saw a tank. "Why can't anybody just honor their word, still risking the safety of others, you don't want me to finish my story!" He looked around for a bit, and then said, "I'm ready to go to jail, come on and take me in. He looked at the camera on his phone and said, "I love you mom, I can't apologize, my siblings should never have to go through this, nor should anybody else, this is for them". He looked up at the sky, and said, "I'm coming to join you Trey". For the first time, an emotion appeared, and a tear rolled down his face.

The SWAT team moved in slowly proceeding with caution. Quincey got down on his knees refusing to lay face flat, but kept his hands balled up but placed behind his back. The SWAT team was so relieved to arrest him, that they just removed the items from around his neck, and done a quick pat search. They slow walked him down to a paddy wagon, and right before they stopped, Quincey squeezed down on the button in his hand. The sound from the explosion was like a mini atomic bomb going off, that only made it worse by causing the other nine squad cars to disassemble on both sides of the street and rained down like igneous rocks from a volcano. Some people were trying to peek out of their windows, but were frightened by the violence of an explosion.

CHAPTER 9

Stacy had just started to doze off waiting on this guy to turn himself in, who Quincey had mentioned to her, but she couldn't fight it any longer. She was awakened by her cellphone constantly ringing. "Hello", she answered with a dry voice. "Oh, hold on", she said turning her TV to the 24hour fox news. "I got it, let me call you back Kat. Thank you". She hung up grabbing some pillows throwing them on the floor getting a closer look at the news. "Mmm, you telling me all this time he was the guy turning his self in. Unbelievable". She started to massage her scalp, still in disbelief, she just stared at the television, "I wonder if..." And before she could even finish, she grabbed her phone looking to see if Cindy's number was still in her phone. When she found it, she hit the send button. Not even prepared on how to start such a conversation off, she closed her eyes hoping that no one answered, but they did. "Yeah?" said a tired voice, "I hope this is important" Stacy knew from how she answered, she couldn't have known or she'd probably be on the phone herself with Quincey's mother. "Hello". Cindy said one more time. "I'm sorry but, I just got a call myself telling me to turn to the 24hour fox news station, and it was Quincey, Ms. Williams, and I don't know his mother's name..." "No, no, no, no please no. God don't let this happen again, please don't". Stacy just waited patiently cause it already seemed as if Cindy already had somewhat of a clue as to what may of happened. "Sorry", Cindy said searching for her remote control almost scared to find out if that was in fact Quincey. Nervous, her hand trembled as she fought with the power button on the remote control. When the news appeared on the screen, it wasn't giving her enough to go on, she couldn't function, her vision started to blur. Her body started to do a whole lot of foreign things almost causing her to hyperventilate. Cindy felt her phone vibrate for about a brief second, so she knew it was a text message she didn't really want to open up, but she didn't have much of a choice. It read:

"I know this may come as a bigger shock to you then it has to me because you are his family, but I was wishing that it wasn't him as well when I received the call. I apologize for having to deliver this news like this, but he live streamed it. I may not be able to help much, but if you need someone to talk to, I can be available for you".

Cindy sent back a thank you text. She tampered with her phone until she found what it was that she was looking for. At the sight of what she saw, almost caused her to throw up as she became nauseous. She turned away from the picture trying to gather herself, fighting with her belief not wanting it to be the person she was just looking at commit the disgusting act that she'd just witnessed. "Not my nephew", she whispered mustering the strength to hold back her tears, "No Quincey, no", she whined. She didn't want to watch it anymore, but something inside of her urged her to watch the entire video. The clock on her wall read 2:49 a.m. to be exact, and she knew that Karmen knew nothing about this because she hadn't called or come over. She was afraid to call her because she already knew what the felling was like to lose a son, but this was no ordinary case of losing a loved one at the hands of the police, "our government", this was her son taking his own life along with the same individuals who were normally responsible for killing someone's son and not the other way around. She finished watching the horrific video trying to grasp comprehension to know just it was her nephew was going through, and refused to talk to them about.

"Call Karmen". Karmen had been sitting downstairs in the dark since 1:30 a.m., beyond angry. She couldn't really sleep feeling as if something was wrong, and just as she suspected, when she went to go and check on the children, Quincey was the only one not there. She decided not to call him and just wait for him to just sneak in, but she was beginning to really worry herself when she kept hearing the loud thunderous sounds at that time of the morning. She didn't want to cut on the television in fear of what might appear. She thought to give it just a few more minutes knowing she had to go to work soon. She got up, looked out the kitchen curtains, didn't see anyone so she tried the front. Coming up empty, she went upstairs and check her own room is when she saw her phone vibrating lighting up. She reached for it seeing Cindy's picture and answered, "Girl what you doing up this late?" "A bad call, open the door, I'm coming over". She didn't even allow Karmen to ask any questions by hanging up right away. When

Cindy made it over there, she walked in the door with pajamas and sneakers on raising a red flag in

Karmen's mind. "Girl...what got you up at this time of morning in pajamas and sneakers?" Cindy said, "Hold on girl, let me catch my breath, and pour us a drink". She pulled two decent size glasses from out of the kitchen cabinets, and then reached underneath the bottom cabinets and grabbed whatever bottle came first. She poured until the glasses were about full, until Karmen who had been standing there with her hands on her hips, said, "What could be this exciting that you done filled them glasses up like that?" "Get you a seat and drink!" She trusted Cindy, but she figured she could use a drink anyway while her nerves were still unsettled awaiting her son's return. Cindy would drink, and then steady Karmen eyes to see if she was buzzed yet, it didn't look it, so she poured some more. Half way through that glass, Karmen became inpatient and jumped up, "Alright, what the fuck is going on, now I've been waiting on Quincey to bring his ass home so I can lay him out, and then you come over here quiet, pouring drinks. I don't want another drink, tell me..." "Quincey dead baby". Cindy just blurted it out not knowing how to really say it. "Bitch don't play wit me". That was the one news Karmen never wanted to hear was that of her children had to be buried. "I know, I...let me show you, you have to sit Karmen, please". It was as if all of her energy had drained from her body anyway, when she understood that Cindy wasn't about to take back what she had just told her, and the fact that her facial expression hadn't changed. "Please God don't allow this to keep happening to us, we are not bad people....noooo". At that moment she started to break down, Cindy helped her up to the couch where she laid her head on her shoulder, and the two of them cried together. All of this noise had awakened the twins, that no one heard them coming down the steps. "What's going on?" Robbin asked as Robert started from a mind state of confusion. "Your brother's gone baby. Quincey's...gone". Robbin walked slowly over to the love seat and asked, "Where did he go?" "He's...dead baby". It was no other way to dress it up, and it hurt even more to spew those words out of her mouth to children. Robbin broke down into a quite sob, whereas Robert didn't know what he should do as the new man of the house, should he go and console his mother, or his sister since they were spaced apart. So he pulled his sister's hand, pulling her to her feet hugging her, and then walked her over to where his mother was sitting so they could all bond in togetherness. "Aw babies, I'm so sorry...mommy didn't do enough. I could of been a better mother...maybe I didn't talk to him enough. I told him not to leave out of here...why didn't he listen, why?" "Karmen honey, don't do this to yourself, you are a great mom, look at me...don't never let me hear you discredit yourself, and we'll have this conversation at another time...but sweetie, his mind was already made up". Karmen didn't know how to suppress everything that she was feeling at the moment, so she just sprung up from the couch and headed for the kitchen. "Who wants something to eat? I'm a make some breakfast". Cindy got up heart broke from looking at the twins and went into the kitchen to help Karmen calm down. "Come on baby, here, come on and sit down. I'll cook, I got it". Karmen couldn't help but notice Cindy's phone sitting right in front of her, but it was the image on the screen that caught her attention. "This what you wanted me to see?" "You don't have to see it now, take your time baby, just..." "No, I'm a look at it now", she said through sniffles. She started the video from the beginning, and was quite shocked at what she seen. "My baby didn't do that...nope", she said shaking her head. "They trying to make him out to be some type of bad guy..." "No baby, I watched the whole thing, and when you hear his reason why, he's been trying to tell us this the whole time". Karmen put herself through the agony to watch the full length of the video. She was on the brink of breaking down again when she saw them placing her child under arrest, and then she was uneasy when she couldn't see him anymore, but could hear the sound of things exploding. "What...what's going on?" she looked on in desperation for an answer, but got none. "You'll have to catch the news for it, the newspaper reporter told me about this, so I didn't finish looking at 'fox' ". Karmen cut the TV on while she pondered on the unknown.

"I am here right now at the scene of what has to be the most terrific times to date, here in Harrisburg, Pennsylvania. Tim? Are you there?" "Yeah I'm here". "Okay Tim, because I need for you to split the screen so the people can see the aftermath of

a...I don't even know how to describe it Tim. Now this young man named Quincey Whittaker, he was only seventeen years of age, and as I understand it, he was an outstanding young man with a bright future ahead of him. But looking at his precious interviews, and this video he did the live streaming of, you could, and now Tim, I don't want to place my own words in the mouth of yet another person, but it sounded as if he was beyond fed up. As of right now, the death total is fifty three, and I don't believe they are finished. But Tim, we had to believe that this day would soon come, and I could lose my job for saying this, but that was just dumb on their behalf to keep flagging off the very people that you are responsible for murdering, and covering up as justifiable. I mean, a levee only holds so much water as do pressure to a pipe. And Tim I got a tell you, I feel really bad for the young man, he hadn't even lived life, and to endure so much in so little...I'm hurt by this".

The news anchor dabbed at her eyes and continued on, "Tim my job may be gone off after this, but I can't help the way I feel. You put somebody, so young, in a situation like this to attempt to solve a

prevalent problem that not even our very own president tried to solve. Yes I am talking to you Mr. Trump! They are just worried about everything except for what's going on right here in our very own backyard. These young African men and women are hurting here. They have the worst education, the worst jobs, living conditions, you name it. There is no funding to help them achieve their goals and get ahead, but you got funding for the next campaign that's pocketed, or wasted on paper signs and commercials no one really wants to see. Tim we have a lot of homeless people, but they make sure that people that are not of this country have housing, and a loan that they don't have to pay interest on, but they sure create a bunch of bogus programs funded by the Federal government where they can just scheme off the top and all of the president's filthy rich friends can put right in their pockets. I'm serious Tim, I was telling you the other day about my friend who happens to be African American, who I went to college with, they tried to make a criminal out of her until I showed up and they recognized me. Look around you Tim, the people who own everything over here are from other countries, most of who send money back to buy guns and support movements. I'm sorry to vent like that, but this young man just needed someone he could confide in and they would help, but the only thing that this country helped with, was keeping the Africans at the bottom. But Tim, this young man had to blow himself up, and what may be fifty two police officers, to get everyone's attention, other than that, we wouldn't even be discussing the deeper problems that this nation is faced with everyday but choose to ignore". Karmen cut the TV off holding her head up with her hand. When Cindy looked back to tell the twins to come and eat, she saw Robbin standing there leaning against the entrance of the kitchen. "How long you been standing there". Robbin didn't say anything, but she heard the news anchor from the time her mother had turned on the TV. She walked over and placed her arms around her mother's neck and said, "I love you mommy", and those words right there seemed to make things a whole lot better. As she did not want the babies to see her in a weakened state of mind, she needed to be strong having no help with Darnell in prison. "Come on baby". Her daughter sat on her lap and laid her head on her shoulder and stated twirling her hair with her finger. "I'll never leave you mommy". "I know princess, go get your brother and tell him to come on and eat". She sighed and got up to get a paper towel to dry her eyes. "Baby girl", Cindy called out in a low voice, "we got to make sure these babies are okay". "I know, believe me I know. I have to call the jail and let them know so Darnell can call me". "He already knows, trust me". Robin went upstairs to find Robert, and when she noticed

he wasn't in his bedroom. She knew he wasn't in the bathroom because the

door was wide open, so she went to Quincey's room and turned the knob to

find Robert balled up on the bed. She climbed on the bed and balled up right

beside him. Cindy had went up to the bathroom knowing that Robbin went

to go get her brother, and neither one of them returned. "Where ya'll at?"

she asked in a low whisper. She checked both rooms, and when she didn't

see them in either, she tried her luck in Quincey's room where she got back

and went to use the restroom. When she got back downstairs, Karmen said,

"Where are..." "Just leave'em there, they hurting pretty bad". Karmen got

up from the table and went to check on the kids, and when she saw her

babies lying there like two wounded cubs, she laid down and covered them

with her arms as far as they could reach, and blanketed them with the love

that only a mother could distribute.

Cindy was sitting there with her drink and heard Karmen's phone

vibrating from the living room. She went to get it and saw the caller ID's

location and knew that it was her brother. Soon as she accepted it, she was

fooled with a million questions, "Slow down baby, this is your sister...All I

saw was the live streaming video basically saying why he did it...We knew

something was wrong cause his demeanor started to change, and, I don't

know if it was when them cops jumped'em that he just snapped, I don't

know...she upstairs laying down with the kids, hold on". She took Karmen

the phone and went back downstairs. "Hey baby", he could tell that she had

been crying. "Damn, ain't a damn thing I can do from here!" "Baby it's a lot

to take in, especially after I just watched it, up until he blew...himself...up".

Her voice trailed off. "Who...I mean how did he even get his hands on..."

"Darnell...baby...please, I know, but we got to focus on getting you home.

We need you...this is too much to deal with. I pleaded with him not to go there while it was late cause it was too much going on out there". "Where are the kids baby?" "Here ya'll, talk to daddy for a minute". "Hi daddy", Robbin said but not sounding like her normal self, she sounded a lot less enthused. "Talk to me pumpkin, tell me my baby's okay?" "Yes" " You got to be strong..." "Daddy...when you...coming home?" "I'm working on it sweetheart?" "I wish daddy could hold you right now". "I miss you daddy". "I know baby, daddy misses you too, give your brother the phone and go get your Aunt Cindy for me I'm a see if she'll drive ya'll up here, can you do that baby girl?" "Kay". "Hey big man, how you holding up?" "I'm doing okay", he answered in a sad voice. "Damn baby boy, ain't nothing I can say or do". "Hm mom". Robert wasn't in any type of mood to talk, so he handed his mom the phone. When Cindy got upstairs, she asked, "Darnell wanted me?" Karmen handed her the phone, "Okay, soon as the visits open up, we'll be out front".

They finally got passed the front desk at the visitor's room, and waited for Darnell to come out. Soon as his daughter saw that walk of his, she knew that was her father. Robbin leaped up like a gazelle and ran into his arms. Soon as the correctional officer saw it, he felt the need to pester him about it and called him to the desk. "Inmate Whitaker, please report to the officer's desk immediately". He had a funny feeling in the pit of his stomach, due to the previous run ins he had with this guard who always had a racist joke that he wanted you to hear as if he was competing for a comedy gig. When he finally approached the desk, he said, "What's the problem officer", never using the guard's name knowing that kind of pissed him off. "You know you can't be having these rug rats running around here..." "Who the fuck is you referring to as a rug rat..." "Don't be getting all lippy with me gotdammit,

I'll have your visit terminated every time you come out here. I know your son did that to them officers!" Karmen saw the commotion between the two and walked up to the desk. But no one seen the white shirt coming. "Don't ever say my son's name out of your mouth, matter of fact, call a white shirt out here cause you are very disrespectful and need to be dealt with". "What's wrong baby?" Karmen asked tugging Darnell's arm. "I'm...not...calling...a...mutha fucking thing. Remember what I told you. Every last one of you monkeys'll be up out of here..." "Monkeys?" "Who is it that you was referring to using monkeys as the description?" "All no LT, I was joking about the kids running about and carrying on, that's all". The officer made his plea hoping he wasn't caught. "File a grievance when you get back to the block, enjoying your visit, I'll take care of this". "Thank you LT.", Darnell said headed for his seat. The lieutenant stayed at the officer's desk as he waited for another officer to relieve him of his duty. When the visit was terminated, Cindy asked, "What was all of that about?" "Honey, that C.O. tried to say some racist stuff, and got to talking about monkeys..." "Girl who?" "Yeah...talking about us. You know how Robbin ran when she saw Darnell?" "Yeah". "Well, he was tripping on that, but he said something about Quincey, but I missed it, that Lieutenant right there, just listening".

When they got back, Cindy said, "I'm a go in here and wash some clothes and be over later, kay?" "Alright, I'll just leave the door unlocked". When Karmen made it through the front door, she picked up the mail looking through, and saw an envelope addressed to her by Quincey. "Nah, I know I ain't tripping", she cut on the lights and held the envelope up to the light, "Yeah that's him, and it's only dated from two days ago". Just as she going upstairs, her phone began vibrating and she couldn't see who it was because it was in her purse. She put the mail down on the bed and reached in her purse and pulled out her phone and answered. "Oh, I'm looking at ya picture now as I just put it on the speaker. "You ain't gone believe this", Karmen said looking down at the envelope again almost afraid to open it. "Well you first", Cindy said knowing that if she had received a letter, then she knew Karmen had gotten one, but she to didn't want to open hers just yet. "I got this letter from Quincey, and I'm afraid to open it". "Me to girl, it's still unopened, I'll be over when I'm done washing". "Alright, door's unlocked". Karmen saw that she had a bunch of missed calls and text messages, so she started going through her phone to see who she would call back first. When she saw that KJ and Gerald had called, she called them first. "Hey". "How are you holding little sister?" Gerald asked with great concern in his voice. "We just came back from seeing Darnell, I'm keeping it together, besides him, I still got two little ones to grow, so I got to". "I hear that", Gerald said, "I'm a let Kevin talk to you, but if there is anything, I mean anything, you just give us a ring". "Thank you".

"A Karmen, we called soon as we heard. We here for you. Oh, and we got some good news too, their giving us a bail hearing Monday and the DA's not really trying to argue, especially after what just happened, but to play it safe, we got everything laid out, but we're getting ready to go back up in here in this court room and handle business". "Alright ya'll, I appreciate it, and thank you two". "No doubt". She went and checked on the twins to see how they were holding up since the visit, cause everybody's spirits seemed to be up since then. "How you holding up baby", she said to Robert knowing the longer he stayed down and out, so would Robbin and she didn't want to be walking around in a miserable house.

Chapter 10

She waited patiently for Cindy to hurry up who seemed to be taking too long. *"What could be taking that girl that long, and what could she be washing and it ain't but just her there?"* Cindy finally walked through the door clutching the letter written to her by Quincey close to her chest. *"A ya'll, where your mom?"* *"Upstairs"*. When she entered Karmen's room, Karmen was still looking through her phone, seeing who all she still needed to call, when she looked up seeing Cindy standing there smiling. *"Why are you just standing there smiling?"* *"Cause"*. She stood there with her hands on her hips, and said, *"I don't need a reason to smile, you should try it girl, I can't afford to be walking around depressed"*. *"I hear that, want me to go first, alright sit down"*. Karmen didn't wait on a response, she was going to read her letter first regardless. *"Alright, she took a deep breath, and exhaled"*.

"Dear Mom,

By the time that you find the strength to read this correspondence addressed to you, I pray that you are passed the stages of tears, and I ask that while you are on the front row at my funeral, that you shed none, but smile, because what took place was not your fault. The reason why is the reason you are reading this, so I'll get right to it. I made preparations to make sure that you and the family never struggle, so I sold all of my baseball cards, and basketball cards that I possessed, and kept the football cards to pass on to Robert, something dad taught me.

As bad as I felt for leaving my family. I have no regrets. What I've learnt from you and dad, I made it work for me. In order to lead a nation, one must be willing to do, so I pulled my gloves off, and got my hands dirty. If you are mad at me, I know you, you will forgive me soon enough, but I cannot, and will not apologize for my actions. I love you far and beyond, no depth deep enough to cover that. But my promise to you is that I will love you dying to my death and even from the grave. You will remain that special to me. I know you are waiting for me to explain, give me time to formulate. Trevon's death done a lot to me, and for me. It woke me up mom. For all of black folks lives, we've been taught to don't talk back to Mr. Charlie, oh no, you can't do this, don't do that. We fear these people and never were we slaves except in our own mines.

But it's been taught to us, through them, that came before us. The thing about me, like Trevon, neither one of us inherited that fear of the white man, that's a trait that wasn't in my genetics. The amount of time that I had doing research, I learned probably more than a third of the world. And I say that, because of my actions. Have anybody ever learned anything, if they haven't utilized any of the knowledge that they've obtained for the good of mankind? Even in the books in the Bible, it speaks about the punishment of God's chosen people for generations to come, for the actions of our ancestors.   It spoke about our history being scattered as were we, and being forgotten. Anyway, the new day has started to take form. God is restoring us back to our rightful place, which is the throne. We've been through torture trying to make it, yet oppressed and murdered trying to please those who don't respect us. Look at how we live. We don't own much, we work for them, spend our money with them, if you own too much, they tax it. I was fed up, I done seen too much in too little of time. But the experience of seeing it up close, where they just murdered your best friend in front of you, and you see what it's like to really be black through the eyes of the enemy. I couldn't continue to live my life now, tomorrow, and the day after, that this same act will happen to somebody else just like me, if not me. No different than Nat Turner, it needed to be some order, and once he set the stage, the whites panicked killing their own slaves to scare them against the act of rebelling, and it worked. That courageous act could have ended slavery then. Who would want you living on their plantation if they thought them and their family could wake up dead tomorrow? My point, but it humbled the rest of the slaves.

It's the same as today, they murder us screaming justifiable homicide when don't nobody even be armed. How many times do we have to attend our own funerals? Let them see how it feels to miss little Rebecca, or Billy, put them on a R.I.P. T-shirt. They continue this manner of genocide, because they don't know what it's like for a black cop to kill their children every day, or flood their neighborhoods with guns, and narcotics and slump one of them on a regular. They walking around clutching their purses and locking doors every time they see you coming up the street. Right! They got the world thinking they scared of us, but we the ones getting killed. Everything that I did, was to send the correct message, but only to the correct people". "I caught you, and sent you to the same place you sent them". That's what needs to happen every time they squeeze that trigger. But I want to apologize to the world that this hasn't happened a lot sooner. You got one life, and so you live it, but do you live it to die for the cause, or do you live in silence killing the cause? The cause didn't die on my watch mom, I didn't let it. No child should ever fear those who are paid to protect them because they do not like the color of your skin. If they were the good Christian people they professed to be, then how did they miss the part where Noah's seeds birth these nations that include the European race. For many years, European forced the world to believe that they are heirs of the deities, and every race came from them. We gave birth to it all. They struggle with the truth, they did it with the fake Jews. Everybody and their mother should know there was no such thing as a white Jew. Moses was a Jew, and if you couldn't tell the Jews apart from the Egyptians, then would the Egyptians too be white when everybody knows the Egyptians were black. They forced us to pray to a Jesus which is Greek, there were no J's in the old

English dictionary, and no one ever told Hitler he was killing the wrong people. But you see how America gave the survivors reparations having nothing to do with Hitler's actions, gave them a memorial based in New York, when we still trying to get Ms. Harriet to appear on a stamp or a twenty dollar bill, and the only thing they did, by pretending to be funny, was by putting Abraham Lincoln on a brown penny worth one cent. No other race can produce black babies, none. We are the CHILDREN OF GOD! PERIOD! Every time that these spiteful people wake up, and not respect that every day is a beautiful day to die, and believe it, always remember me. It is way more of us on the planet then there are them, then imagine if all of them, like me, responded by answering the bell. But we are not a hateful people, we weren't taught to be that but seems to be our weakness. But look at nature, and animals, and insects. Even a plant will murder you if you cross it. Dog eat dog. The jungle is filled up with animals that kill their own kind, but us, we are a loving people, and the only ones we will kill, is ourselves, shout out to Willie Lynch for teaching us how to hate each other so master always had a snitch to rat out the others. But if I didn't let the world ever change and it would be noted in the history archives as a selfish act of some nut case looking for attention. But you know what they won't do that they do with the white boys who kill up everything? Cut up parts of my brain and do scientific research. You notice that every time white people commit these type of acts, they look for a reason to justify their actions, but they never attempt to see if the brother man is ever competent or not to stand trial, they just feed you to a predominately white, or all white juniors. The human body is no different than a pipe, too much pressure contained by anything will eventually burst. I don't want my brother and sister having these same kinds of encounters growing up, they still have a lot of life to grow. When Trevon died, we were all searching for the answers to the reason of why. Well, I am the answer. I have mailed off two videos that should be aired any day now. So a phone call will be made to you some time soon. I need you pay close attention so you understand".

"I love you beyond life mommy, give my siblings a kiss and a big hug for me, let my dad know I love him so much, and I know he'll be free sooner than he think. Give Aunt Cindy my love and a big hug, let her know I appreciate everything. The two of you take care of one another. I can see her smiling now, cause I know she's there while you are reading this letter, ain't she?

Remember, the video, I love you all. Quincey

Also, attached to the back of this page is a check."

Karmen didn't know how to react to the letter, she just needed a moment, because regardless of what was written in the letter, her son was dead and gone, so the letter became momentous as a souvenir. Cindy awaited patiently allowing Karmen to take in the moment before she read her letter. Karmen took a deep breath, exhaled, and said *"Okay girl, open it up".* "Alright, alright...dag."

"Dear Aunt Cindy,

Knowing that you are already sitting there with my mother, that means that she has already shared her letter with you, and so, I can just skip all the other stuff. First I want to apologize if you believe that I've manipulated you by going to the studio that morning. That was not my intentions, however, I do not want you to, in anyway feel guilty in any type of way. The less you knew, the better off you were. And to be honest, nobody knew what was going to happen. But what I need for you to know, is we didn't lose. You can sleep at night knowing that "I" chose to do something impactful that would not only demand respect for my people, but set the bar as far as no longer allowing those who have malice in their heart to portray the role of the bully. We were never a people to be pushed around, and man handled by weak individuals whose self-esteem is or has been diminished. We represent "power", it's no secret as to why God has chosen us to lead. Being as though our history has been scattered amongst the earth, throughout the very four corners of it we tend not to remember, or know it because of the time period being held captive or in bondage. The slave mentality is what's been holding us back from where we are supposed to be. An Institutionalized mind set, is the reap from the labor of the slave master's sowing. He has been rewarded with us doing the work for them while they sit back and expanded their bank accounts. If you note, we are the only race who will provide a better future for the outsider, before making sure that your brother's future is already secured. I could not allow myself to be at the bottom, in that same barrel amongst the crabs still pulling each other down. Me and Trevon made a promise to return to the community, and help those who live the struggle, once we made it. We were destined to be, and then a tragedy snatched it all away, and the cop didn't really have a clue as to why he had done it other than his pride was hurt. I personally had this conversation with him up close and in person, so it became personal to me, to make sure that he went serving a purpose. To hear the words that was spoken to me was chilling as if puddles of ice were spewing from his mouth each time he expatiated. My bad, you always grind me up for using fancy words, but what good would it do to know them and never use them. Anyway, I couldn't share my ideals with either of you because you would of thought I was either crazy, and try to talk me out of it. This day was destined to happen one way or the other. Revelation spoke about race riots in the coming days, nothing much to be alarmed about, just the fear of the hateful many understanding that their time spent in power is finished. The fear is them being equal to, or less than those that they hated, the same fear, there from, when Lincoln freed the slaves. Power kept a lot of hateful people above water, now imagine what they would do without it. The societal atmosphere that we breath from, is a brain washed society that refuses to expand the brain capacity to better ourselves,

"This is like an episode that continues to get deeper and deeper. Why did this have to happen to us, I mean we're both good people aren't we?" Cindy started to tear up, so to prevent from crying all over again, Karmen thought that she would lighten the mood, and in a cheerful mood said, "Girl, he said it's a check attached to the back!" "I ain't thinking bout no check, I'd rather have my baby back". "Ain't that the truth, but I don't want to be sad no more, that takes ten or fifteen years off your life". "It don't take no ten...who told you that?" "Nobody, it's how I be feeling". Karmen peeled the check from the tape attached to the back of the letter, and just stared at it with her mouth hanging wide open. "What, what, what it say with your mouth opened like that?" Karmen showed Cindy the check so she could see the reason why her mouth was wide open. "Oh my...where the hell all..." "He said he sold some basketball, and baseball cards, and they probably from the old ones his dad gave'em when he was little". "But for two and a half million dollars though? "You got one, what it say?" Cindy slowly turned the page of the letter over, and peeled the check from the tape. She couldn't believe it, it wasn't as near as the amount that Karmen had received but then again she had children and a husband, but it was a lot of money that she didn't have. "What girl, let me see". She turned the check around for Karmen to see it, and they both simultaneously said, "What are you going to do?" Karmen said, "Well you know I still got those two", she said pointing downstairs, "And then Darnell is getting ready to come home any minute, so I'll rather look at a house together, we mind as well move in a decent neighborhood that way we are close to each other". "I don't know if I got it like you". "You better stop playing, that check say three hundred and fifty grand!"

"Jeff!" his mother yelled up the steps, "You got a letter down here, I put it on the dining room table for you". "Okay mom, thank you". Jeff had been sitting in his room since he'd gotten home from school, thinking about what he would say to Quincey's mom once he entered the house. It would be hard to hide the fact that he had any involvement in what resulted in her son's death. This was unlike the death of his biological father, whom he had no real emotional connection to, he actually loved Quincey as a real brother. He gathered himself and walked downstairs straight into the dining room and retrieved the letter. He had picked it up with no idea as to who would be writing him. He thought it might be a love letter, or some type of correspondence from Savannah until he turned it over seeing the name on it. A fully developed teardrop rolled from his left cheek just that quickly as he started to reminisce about the good times they had. He grabbed a napkin from off the table and dabbed at his eyes going into the living room. "Mom, can I use your car for a short moment?" "Use my car for...where are you going?" Over to Quincey's to pay my respect. I won't be long, I hadn't even called his mother yet.

His mother liked Quincey a lot, so when she saw the news, she was deeply saddened. "Let me grab a jacket and my purse, I'll go over there with you honey". When Jeff reached to knock, the door was already opening as Cindy was on her way out. "Oh, hi honey, Karmen", she turned and yelled up the steps. Cindy invited Jeff and his mother in and waited on Karmen to come down. "Hi Robbin and Robert, sorry for your lost. This is Quincey's younger siblings mom". "How are you holding up?" Just as she was reaching to shake their hands, Karmen came down the steps. "Hey Jeff". "Hi Ms. Karmen, I wanted to come over a bit earlier, but I just..." "I understand baby, it's alright". When he broke away from the embrace, he said, "This is my mother..." Not giving Jeff time to say her name, she extended her hand and said, "Hi, I'm Sandy, and I give you my deepest condolence. Oh I just loved Quincey as you and Jeff were very close". "Oh, and the same to you for your lost as well", Sandy was still holding on to Karmen's hand not knowing what exactly to say next, she said, "I know I don't know you all well enough to offer a hand with anything, but if I can help with anything, I mean anything, you just give me a call. Do you have anything to write with?" She felt that the only way she was going to get her hand back was to go and get her a paper and pen. "That's really sweet of you Sandy, and if you need a hand with anything, or even just to talk, you let me know, just give me a call". After speaking to Jeff and his mother for a while, they decided to finally leave, Karmen walked them to the door and promised to call sometime.

CHAPTER 11

Diamond had been continuously crying from a mixture of Quincey's death and hormones that her emotions were all over the place. She remained in a fetal position in her bed not understanding why he would just up and decide to leave them like that. "He just left us...this wasn't supposed to happen like this...it wasn't", she said in a voice just below a whisper, "We were gonna be a family, we were gonna surprise him". Diamond had gotten the mail off of the floor when she came in the door from school, at the sight of seeing Quincey's name after hearing the gossip about the incident responsible for his demise, her and the letter had been laying on the bed since then. She knew she couldn't lay there forever wishing that the hurting would stop, she needed to be strong for this baby to grow healthy inside of her. She finally found the inner strength to get up out of the bed, and once she finished reading the letter that Quincey had written to her, she would tell Ms. Karmen the news in person. She stared at the envelope still unable to process what was happening, she took a deep breath, "Okay girl, you can do this". She slowly opened the letter shaking her head, "You got this girl".

"Dear Diamond,

I really don't even know how to start this letter because I know that you are very upset with me as you read this correspondence. You will always be my Diamond in the rough as we began different journeys, from the time this letter ends, until the moment that you finish reading. The secret that you believed you were hiding from me, I already knew about it. I didn't say anything because I didn't want to complicate things even more with the issues already overcrowding my plate. I know it sounds selfish, but my mind was already made up. I don't ask anyone to try and understand because my intentions were not done for me, but for we. That seed growing inside of you should never have to watch a best friend, or anyone who resembles him or her, getting murdered in cold blood because the belief of another who at many time decides to play God. My seed should not have to live in fear. I saw the pregnancy test, but the one lesson that life teaches us, is you can't avoid destiny. I need you to believe that I would never just up and leave you, you deserve to be Queen. Even though I may not be present physically to enjoy a life with you and our child, but I will always be there spiritually, that part of me is eternal. Please don't hate me, but allow yourself to be comfortable with the idea of why I did it was for the greater of good. I would never turn my back on my family without the cause being greater than. I know that it is impossible for you to see the reason why I done what I did with a blurred vision, but hopefully later on in the future that you or our child has to experience the same encounters that me, or someone close to you has experienced. These memories of what they have done to us will always remain, even after I am gone, it's a scar that's deep. I sent a video to a journalist with instructions that I trust, she will contact my mom and inform them when the video will be ready for air. From that point on, you'll have better clarity and understanding. I know that I can't make you feel any better with words alone, and I won't be able to bring me back once it's all over, but I ask that you trust in the process. You get to tell our beautiful baby girl, or boy, but I know you'll have a girl, but whatever God blesses one with is fine. But you get to tell her, or him, the reason why once that question is asked of where daddy. I apologize to place such a burden on you, but I know you will do a great job explaining, you're gonna be a beautiful mother and I wish that I could be there for the two of you and make things right, but unfortunately not. When our child is old enough, there is a DVD player in my room with a disc already in it, that is for our child. I don't want to be too long because I know it's painful, because it's very painful for me to write *you this letter. This will be the worse thing that I've ever done in my life, and that's walking away from you and my family, and I know that deep down in my heart it comes off as selfish, but I swear to you, what I believe in me, then you should trust and believe in me still. I love you with everything Diamond, and I know the number one question is why didn't I stay. Each individual will have their own destiny to fulfill in life, and he forced to make a decision that dictate the lives of many others, but whose to say what's really right or wrong when judging you along your life's path, the first thing that a parent does, whether an animal or a human being, they protect their young even if it means to die for. I want you to know that I appreciate you, and will love you even after my time here is up.*

I apologize cause the last thing I want to do is end this in such a way, but it has to be done. Don't forget to check my DVD player. Sealed with all the love I can give, and pray that you don't hate me after reading this.

Attached to the back is a check that can help with some financial struggles that you may run into down the road. I still want you to attend college as promised, and know that my mother will be there for you one hundred percent of the way knowing that I left a part of me behind. She always thought you and I made a power couple. Sorry my love, but I have to go, but I promise to find you again in the next life time.

Always and forever,

Quincey"

Diamond was staring at the letter as if it was talking to her as she was reading it. She pressed the letter hard to her chest and hugged the pages as if it were Quincey himself. Her cry was about as soft as a kitten's when separated from his mother. When she finally got up, she almost forgot, and turned over the last page of the letter to see that he had indeed attached the check as promised. When she saw the five zeros after the first five, her mouth went to the floor as she couldn't believe it wondering where he had got the money from knowing Quincey was a square kid. She had tucked the letter away in her dresser draw along with the check, and called a cab. "Yes, can I please have a cab?" She gave her address and the location that she was going and waited.

Jeff decided to open his letter once he got in the house and made it to his room for a little bit of privacy. He shut his door and opened the letter, it read:

"Dear Jeff,

I know you have some questions as to how things ended, and so I'll try and answer as best as I can. I didn't share with you the rest of my plans, because they no longer included you. I was trying to protect your future in keeping you from any troubles that may follow, or catch up to you in the days to come. You know as well as I, these people don't believe anyone not European to be intelligent enough to carry out a plan using strategies that make them look like clowns, and so they would have used every available resource within their reach to find out if I was alone or with someone when carrying out these acts. You done more than enough, and I honestly appreciate you for being a real friend. You can't search the planet and find one or two people like yourself to help move a mountain in dire times like this. These coming days are going to be dreadful and chaotic where people of all racial ethnic backgrounds may have to pick a side. In the mean time, spend more time with your mother before you start to attend college. She's a very good woman, and you only get one mother, do the best you can to keep a smile on the little lady's face. I hope everything heals with time and the both of you find peace of mind along the way on your journeys. I will try and keep this short and simple being as though you already knew my reason in all of this from the beginning, so it's no need for me to keep continuously explaining myself.

Just make the best out of you, in case you want to do something special for yourself, or buy Savannah something. Treat her well, and all ends the same, you never know, she could be the one.

But listen man, I respect you to the fullest, I wish nothing but the best for you and yours. I made a video explaining my reason why, that I mailed to the journalist who will get a copy to the host on that CBS morning show I appeared on, and from there, distribute it to all of the other news stations. But the journalist will contact my mom and let her know when it will air giving you time to catch it. Don't be sad or shed a tear for me, we made a very big difference.

I love you, and take care. Quincey, B.T.W."

CHAPTER 12

Stacy had been sitting in her office pondering as to whether or not she wanted to look at the video she had received in the mail from Quincey on the job, or at home. When she thought about all of the nosy people who would always peep in her office in attempts to spy on projects she was working on, or to steal bit and pieces of information, she placed the package in her purse and decided to wait until later once she got home to watch in peace. Soon as she got home she decided to call Kathuran up to see if she cared to join her in being the first to see the video. When Kathuran agreed, she went in to the kitchen, fixed herself a bite to eat, and made herself a cocktail. Just as she stepped out of the shower, she heard the doorbell while she was drying her hair and raced to answer it. "Hey Kat". "Hey yourself, I see you must of just stepped out of the shower, I could of caught you at another time". "Don't be silly girl, you know how it is when you come home from work and you want to relax a little". "Well let's go and watch, cause I really would like to hear what he had to say that may of been different from the times that he was a guest on my show, or that streaming situation". "Well, we're about to find out in one second, you want anything before we start?" "No, just a bottled water please". After the video was done, neither of the two spoke a word for a while after taking in everything that Quincey felt was necessary to speak on.

Finally Stacy broke the ice and asked, "So when do you think you can get this in?" "I can make it a special tomorrow, it was going to be a few guest who were mainly going to have a debate about racism, so instead of cancelling them, they can be just of the video and have a debate or just a real intelligent conversation, because I don't really see any room for that". "Yeah, you right about that part, but in the eyes of the racist they will always be right even when they don't make any sense. Well let me call his family so they know when to watch, and what time". "You know that'll be cool if I could get them on the show..." "No, these were in his instructions what not to do so his actions don't put the lives of his family in danger, I'm sure they would prefer to watch from home anyway, so they won't be mobbed by news reporters and hecklers, or some crazed deranged person or people attempting to harm them". "I guess I wasn't looking at it from that perspective, just the conversation part, it needs to be heard, all at once from all sides". "I know what you mean, it's still dangerous though". Stacy called Karmen, and then Cindy, and gave them both the time and day that the video would air.

Jeff decided to send Karmen a text as a reminder that as soon as she got word about the video being aired, to contact him. When the cab pulled up, Diamond paid the driver, got out, and then just stood there for a minute trying to contrive a respectable way to share the news with Karmen knowing she was already in grieving state of mind after just losing her son. "To heck with it, we here now", she said to herself and headed toward the house. She held her breath, and knocked on the door. When the door opened, she said, "Hi Robbin, is your mother home?" "Mom, Diamond is here for you". "How are you two holding up?" she asked sitting in between the twins giving them both a hug. "Hey Diamond" Diamond got up and met Karmen at the bottom step wrapping her arms around her and then breaking down into an uncontrollable sob laying her head on Karmen's shoulder. Even though it was her son, Karmen believed that they all shared the lost of someone special.

She lifted Diamond's head caressing her cheeks and said, "Look at me sweetie, we're gonna be okay, it's alright". "No...it's...not", Diamond spoke in between sobs, "Can...can...I...talk...to...you...in...pri...vate...pl...ease?" "Sure honey, come on". She basically held Diamond up going up the stairs one step at a time. She led her into her bedroom, "and tell me what's wrong, what's the matter huh?" "He just left us, why would he just do that to us?" "I know baby, I know. It's alright, let it all out". "I never got a chance to tell him Ms. Karmen, it was supposed to be a surprise for his birthday, but he already knew, but I wanted to tell him the news". "Wait a minute baby, you loosing me. What was supposed to be a surprise?" Diamond lifted her head up, still without eye contact, and said, "That...that...I", and then her voice trailed off. "Come on baby, you can tell me, I am here for you. Look at me". Again she lifted Diamond's chin to draw eye contact with her. "Your secret is safe with me baby". "I'm pregnant Ms. Karmen". Karmen pushed everything to the side, excited as she was deed down inside to believe that her son had left behind a child, Diamond had to be strong for that reason if nothing else. "Stop it! Look at me baby. We, you and me, are gonna be strong for that little one growing inside of you. You and me love". Diamond locked her arms around Karmen's neck again, but this time even tighter. "Two". "Two what?" Karmen tried removing Diamond's arms from around her neck to look at her when she answered, but was successful. Diamond said, "Two, I am pregnant with twins Ms. Karmen, how am I going to do this by myself?" "Your not, I will be there for you every step of the way". She hugged her back as a mother protecting her young. She smiled to herself silently thanking God, and then kissed Diamond on the forehead. "There", she said, "Your too pretty to be crying. Do your mother know?" "No ma'am she's always away on business". "Alright, well you make sure I have her number before you leave here, you hear?" "Yes". Karmen was so preoccupied with Diamond, that she ignored her ringing cell phone, when she saw the missed call from Stacy, she immediately called her back. "I'm sorry honey, I was in the middle of something important...yes...okay...thank you".

She opened the missed email seeing that it was Jeff, and sent him the information he inquired about. She then called Cindy, "Girl what you doing?" "Cleaning up a little, why what's up?" "Guest what girl, I'm a be a grand-mom child". "Shut up, you ain't..." "Yes I am, and we got twins". "I'm on my way over, you better not be playing". They talked for a while, then dropped Diamond off at home and found a small quiet place to celebrate. Karmen had awakened at 5:30 a.m., which was over a hour ago as the clock in the kitchen read 7:15 a.m. She called Cindy to make sure she was up, and to let her know that she was making breakfast. She had every TV in the house on CBS making sure she didn't miss anything as she tried to keep busy. She called Cindy quick, "You think you could keep an eye on this food for me while I go get Diamond?" "I'm right on the porch". "Ya'll come on and wash up and get ready for breakfast, you only got about forty minutes before that video with your brother Airs". Karmen grabbed her car keys and left out.

Stacy left out of Kathuran's dressing room and walked into the taping area where she saw the two guest who were supposed to do the debating. "Hello, how are you", she said extending her hand, "Johnny right?" "You remember me huh?" "How can I not, you impressed me". The guy sitting right across from the person that she was speaking with, seemed to keep rolling eyes, and shifting in his seat like something was crawling under his skin. "Hello, how are you sir?" When she offered her hand to him, he frowned upon it and turned his head in the opposite direction. "Never mind him, he's been that way since he started thinking, some people never change, but underneath the mask, he's a really good person". "And how would you know?" "Believe it or not, he's a good friend of mines, he might of thought that you was here for the debate. That's Jason Garrit. Apologize to the lady man, she's not here to debate with you". "I apologize if I offended you, I was preparing my game face, it's already hard enough going up against him". He extended his hand, she accepted his apology and asked, "So how do ya'll come up with who debates against who?" "It something that's been going on for years, it just happened, but you want to pick the people who has a sharp intellect but keeps it respectful". Johnny said looking at Jason to see if he wanted to join in or add something to it. "Well, when it's over, no one will be trying to kill one another, and as you can see, we aren't on video Skype". "Okay, is everybody comfortable where they are because we are about to start. Honey make sure you get the best angles when the guest are speaking". "Five, Four, Three, Two, One". "I am your host Kathuran McNeal, and today we have a special story where I will play you a video that was sent to my closest friend Ms. Stacy Fallings", she said pointing at Stacy, "and no, she has nothing to do with anything other than ,making sure that the message gets out, so that everybody get to hear the honest reason why this man...this young man Quincey Whittaker, done what he done. Now I don't want to tell you what my opinion is, but I watched the video...and...you have to see it for yourself". She gave a thumbs up and a picture appeared from the video.

CHAPTER 13

"My name is Quincey Whittaker, and I know there is a lot of people with a whole bunch of mixed feelings. Some angry, some happy, etc..., but I want everybody watching who has formed an opinion, or, who has decided to judge me without full comprehension, to know first hand my reason why. I am not out to change your mind and what you think of me, we're passed those stages. Brought in this world March 5th, 2003, 2:50 a.m. Raised by two loving parents who did everything right, worked hard to provide, three outstanding children, taught to respect those who have come before us as well as after. I had several scholarships to Big Schools, and not because of sports. But this isn't about me, it's about everybody else. We do not live in a world that is deserving of selfish people, the world don't deserve that. When my uncle Leon Williams was shot and killed by some reckless cops as usual they started shooting out with innocent by-standers all around not caring who gets caught in their line of fire. Not one of those officers went to my Aunt Cindy's home, and apologized. They gave them medals. An older guy from my neighborhood named Malcom, known as Montana, cop jogging mysteriously around 2 a.m. when the clubs were closing or shutting down. Hears gun shots from the opposite direction of the victim, and he just happens to have a gun while jogging, pulls his pistol piece and shoots at the people trying to run for cover, and bang. Shot the unarmed man in the head. No one makes a mention that that officer was supposed to call in for back up while being off duty, but instead, he's chasing the people who needs help and murder one. Gave him a metal. My father, arrested for a crime that they knew a white man committed. Darnell Whitaker! I love you daddy", his voice trailed off. "Sean Bell, Eric Garner, Michael Brown, Orlando Castille, Sandra Bland, the incident in Cleveland where

they emptied a hundred and thirty seven bullets in a slow rolling SUV, and the one officer climbed on top of the roof and emptied his clip shooting the female in the top of the cranium execution style. It's a never ending list, those are just names of the top. But if it's me, correct me, I have no problem admitting when I'm wrong, do you? It appears to be a war on blacks and we seem to not of gotten the memo. My cousin Trevon Williams was killed by a cop on the job who was drunk, and his partner Hector DeJesus, knew he had been drinking before they got in the car. Now my cousin is dead cause in this officer's mind, my cousin refused to be like the other niggers on the plantation, who respect masta's wishes. Quincey became irate. The badge protects European cops, or Europeans period, and celebrate them when they kill a nigger. They either get slapped on the hand to never do it again, or they get high praises and medals. This cop got bodies, he done murdered more than a few people, his family, senators and Internal affairs, so every time he kills as a cop, his own family is the one's who investigates and clears him...every time!" He laughed. "But white society looks at these acts as if this shit is normal! If you feared the Afrikan species as you pretend, do you think you would trust that nigger to harvest your crops, to live on your plantation, to drive you around, to feed you, breast feed your children, crack your whip to the back of another Afrikan, and bust ya guns and you still alive. Don't be fool to answer that cause it's not a question. Somehow, people believe that the lies you told when there is no logic in any of them. All of these officer's dead within the last month, never met anyone so deserving of death since I've been alive. And no teenage child should ever feel that way, but I had a one-on-one conversation with that cop, Benjamin Taggart who referred to black people as the shit on the bottom of God's feet. Hector could have ended all of this, by putting an end to the one who initiated this whole domino effect. I put the gun in his hand, and gave him opportunity to end this. The same animal who tried to assassinate the Chief, and missed his target. Hector said he couldn't do it, now he sleeps beneath the earth.

Those cops still missing, it's safe to have the funeral, now their families know how Emmit Tills' family felt. I apologize if I sound cold hearted to my peers, but you have no idea, the adults have done nothing to change the savage ways of the beast. I took up that yoke. Through all of the protesting and marching, long as we didn't riot, everything was cool, cause then it was a bunch of stupid shit black folks making some noise that would never change anything. Well, I'm not marching, and I'm not protesting, I'm returning the favor. Bet I have everybody's attention now. Mainly the one's whose in charge of the country, you are the one's responsible for this, because you always approve of these actions. You created a monster you didn't care to control because you believe it was keeping the niggers in check. Willie Lynch huh? The same act or tactic used on the Indians when you took their land from them, just released all of the savages from the London prisons, who would rape, rob, pillage, murder, spread diseases and so on, you people will stop at nothing to try and be the only existing life on the planet that you already started packing up trying to aim for the moon and mars. Sad. What would you do if you were the only people left? You would either die from boredom or kill each other off through greed, the root of it all. You people are the destruction of humanity, and ignore it for one more dollar that you may never spend. We are the number one consumers in the country, that's over two trillion dollars a year; you get crafty when then wages go up, the price of living go up, and you make up a bogus story about how the cows went on strike at the farm, so now milk is five dollars. Gasoline five dollars, bet you didn't question how we was gonna drive, you try to keep the black people depending on the government keeping us in a perpetual predicament. The sooner as we overcome that obstacle, you kill somebody else sabotaging our growth. I know what you are thinking, but those cops are not dead by accident, and even though no family should have to go through that, no one shows empathy or sympathizes when it's a black person being killed because it is believed to be normal. Time and time again, we have asked that famous question, when will the killing stop? I am tired of seeing Jesse and AL every time one of us are laid to rest. Even when Trevon M. was killed while Obama was in office, they duked us right in our faces, you can't believe that the prosecutors withheld that evidence, where they allowed the guy who owned the gym to lie saying the killer didn't know how to throw an effective punch, then try and bring the evidence in late, where the gym owner was using the killer to promote his gym. Obama, he wasn't no help, they pretend racism don't exist. A lot of it went on in his campaign, and also with his dear friend Dr. Gates. We live in a society that DO NOT hide the racism! Let me ask you some questions white America. Would you like it if I called your children little crackas, and treated them as three fifths of a human being, threw them into bondage, creep into their shed at some time in the morning, raping them for sexual gratification, ravish them for breeding purposes where my own children are also my slaves, and call the lightest of the half breeds, a house nigger, and a house cracka, or if I forced my religion on them, and made them believe in a savior who is never coming, had them worshipping false prophets and idols, and if they refuse or get caught believing in anything other than what I say is law, hang them from those same trees my ancestors hung from, or cut out their eyes because they wanted to read, or if you are disobedient, I rape your son or your daughter in front of you, or sell them to another slave master to separate them from their family, or how about I break me a slave, and put a noose around your husband's neck while beating him unmercifully, and then just cut off his penis and put it in his mouth and set him on fire until burnt to a crisp? I can keep going, but I don't have to be present to see the looks on your faces, you are horrified. This is why I reinvented that same famous act of Willie Lynch on Benjamin Taggart, so that it is branded in the minds of those racist individuals who believe it would never happen to them, no two men bleed any different than the next. Do you see any of these white power groups acting like cowboys in any of them gun carrying states, they would've been dead. They do things *that they know they can get away with, if there was never any outcries, there would be nobody out looking for the killer. America is like a parent raising spoiled children, something like the white kid who got away with killing al them people cause he was driving under the influence, but because he never heard the word no before, they made up a illness called...affluence, or affluent, something to that effect. But the excuses are a pile of bullshit, you can't run around as if you have a legit license to murder at will with no penalties, I think effigy is the best way to describe it. You know as well as I, that Abraham Lincoln never freed slaves because he believed it the right thing to do. He owned about two hundred and seventy, if not more slaves, probably the most in that state. But knowing that, you never changed the text books. Christopher Columbus never discovered anything other than the fact that he had reached puberty. You can't discover something that you already knew was there when the black guy was the one who took him and showed him the Americas where the Indians lived, the same genius who thought the world was square. But again you still teach it. These fifty states of America, for the most part, is stolen land. Then you got the nerve to sell the Mexicans a green card to move back home, the only illegal aliens of foreigners is you! But you don't hear me...that's why those officers are dead, because of what they represented, which is the best. And I apologize to those of you who had to witness my outburst who do not play a part or a role. However, we all need to hold each other accountable for why this country is like it is. Stop voting for who told the most lies, or who promised a tax cut, or who promised to cut crack down on crime when the criminal is them. All you rapper's and actors who have heavy influence, Oprah, Michelle, but with comprehension as to how the politics, govern, white house, etc...., run for the seats, run for that office. Mrs. Obama, Ms. Winfrey, you could have been the first female President and Vice President to make the biggest difference in history period, on a global level. We are responsible for allowing this guy in office now, who inspires people to hate, who adds fuel to any fire. I wonder if* he knows that he is German. You, and I mean black people, if you never stopped for anything, now is your moment, stop trying to make your kids the next Jordan, or Kobe, you sending your children to school to be ball players when the Europeans are sending their children to school to become the next cop who arrest you, the next prosecutor who prosecute you maliciously, and the next judge who sentences you to life as a juvenile. They are to become the next generation of Senator's who passes these bills that target the Afrikan in America. You're not woke, and you still be stuck with that mentality "nothing will ever change". It never does, cause you stay the same, and you know the saying, "nothing changes if nothing changes". You have to activate the other percentages of your brain that you don't use, I'm afraid that we aren't even using the seven or eight percent that the scientist say we do. Stop buying your children what they say is the new trend, it's the new reason you stay broke, you don't need a three hundred dollar pair of J's to go to school and only where them for maybe one month, you make everybody else rich but yourself. The world is just like prison, no one makes money without you, we make the world go round. Every race on the planet is traced back to those Afrikan bones that archaeologist dug up that were older than two thousand years old they named Lucy. So for you racist folk, you are from that same DNA as me, so I am forgiving you because you didn't know due to ignorance, and I am offering you an olive branch for peace so that we can all rebuild this country from scratch and set a real example for the rest of the world to follow. War only leads to destruction , and in the end, no one wins. If anyone asked you why do you hate anybody who is not white, you have a answer. It's sad, but scary. The type of society we live in, you look to guns for power, have you ever looked yourself in the mirror and asked yourself, what would you really do if we lived like the British and had none, would you be who you've become today? Can you honestly look your children in the eyes and explain to them why you hate?" Quincey looked in the camera and said, "What's expected of you shouldn't have to be asked, we are *the worse example to lead a nation, and then we wonder why our children shoot up the schools, another kid, or killed their parents, look at us. This, or these terrible acts that I committed, never has to repeat itself ever, but nor should yours. I challenge each and every one of you to make amends with the neighbors you've hated, promise yourself a brand new start in building a new relationship, teach each, help each other, just be the best person you can be setting the example for the next generations to come. There will be, in the coming days, some people looking to retaliate, trust me, you can learn a lot from a dummy, but just do your research, it's nothing that compares to what my people have been dragged through. Let it go for the sake of good". A tear fell from Quincey's eye as he said, "I wish this didn't have to happen".*

He ended the video, and soon as it was over, the camera crew zoomed in on Kathuran who seemed to be teary eyes even after seeing it already, took a moment to gather her words, "I apologize, but it's just that, that young man had a bright future, I enjoyed his company. But it's sad that all of this had to happen for us to know how bad he was hurting. But...we never know how bad it is until something happens, and he's actually telling the world why he did what he did and what needs to happen so that history don't repeat itself. Who would like to start the..." "I'll go if no one mind", Jason said raising his hand. "Floor is yours". "Thank you Johnny. For those who don't know, I was here for a good debate, I had no idea I would be watching what I just saw. Man...how do you...it's not even a debatable topic". He started rubbing his eyes, and then placed his head in his hands. "Ahem, excuse me. We've been having these conversations for years, and he's right, nothing has changed. There is nothing racist about me, Johnny here will tell you that. We have these debates for good conversations to touch on topics others dare not to get the ball rolling so that people grow into it. I can only apologize for my peoples actions, even though I played no part in any of this. But I mean, despite what's been done, and my heart aches for the officer's families, and the young man responsible. But he's right, knowing how people in this country and other parts of the world treat people, is mainly from seeing how we treat people here. We set the worst examples of them all, I mean we intervene in everybody else business, when we kill more people then all of the terrorist combined. I guess the question is how do we get others who are resistant to the idea of togetherness to be on the same page, I guess we got a great deal of work cut out for us. Go ahead Johnny". "I agree, it's not a debatable one this time, maybe the next time. You know, I grew up as a target who experienced and comprehend how the Europeans created jobs to provide for their families by arresting the minorities for trumped up charged, mistaken identity, even went through a situation where the judge, DA, police officers made up a case in my face while in the court room, because I refused to pay the lawyer who was in cahoots with the prosecutor who would go and work for him in the coming weeks while still litigating the case. So I know how it all works from studying this system. It's not broken. That's a misconception. It isn't made to work for us, you climb over the first hurdle, everybody else follows you for a way out, and then they get road blocked saying they are time barred, it wasn't retroactive, or, the case used wasn't precedent. And the young man made sense, what we need to do instead of ,arching and protesting, is storm the government mansions in every state, storm the oval office, and don't let them spin you, force their hands, spend no unnecessary money that support their businesses, cast not one vote. We got to make them rewrite the whole constitution, make them respect us like it was us who built this country and made it what it is today. Respect me for my peoples is the reason that you are sitting here as a super power!" Johnny pulled out a handkerchief to wipe the beads of sweat from his forehead.

"How could someone look him in the eyes and tell him...he is the. Mmmm. The poop on the bottom of God's feet. But mean it! And he is one of the God's chosen people! Forgive my outburst, but you never know how you feel until you've felt it. It's only so much pressure that can be contained by the pipe before it becomes broken". His voice went low, you could see that he was truly effected by Quincey's delivery. "I am not embarrassed to say that I stand by this young man. Make no mistake, I don't condone the murder of all those people, it came sooner than later. It's been brewing for a very long time, I'm talking Nat Turner long. But what's sad, is we still hadn't found a respectable resolve because people keep acting like nothing has ever happened, or it's nothing happening now. The U.S. of A, gave these, and no disrespect to them cause they don't know they are not Jews. But the U.S. gave these people a place to live, and reparation from something that had nothing to do with the U.S., and here we are, the very people that built this country, and handed you your independence and we having a hard time collecting unemployment, homeless and what not...I feel pain...I hurt right here", he said pounding his chest, "My momma hadn't slept good in years afraid of what I've became when the system had me trapped for a crime I hadn't committed. Called myself rebelling, and played right into their hand; it was rough, but here I stand. It's no different than a drug addict, everybody wants to know why they can't stop. We all have something we love just like the drug addict, and mines was hurting something, jack something, slang something."

"Adrenaline rushes, you get trapped up in your own mind, and you can get lost there forever. I found my way...I need to be a part of this new movement, I wanna help as much as I owe it to people". Stacy was on the verge of tears, she sprung up and gave Johnny a hug, she too came from that type of environment, and people didn't understand the obstacles you had to climb and hurdle over, it was hard, but she made it. But she too wanted to give back in a major way. "I'm with you", she whispered in his ear. She let go and said, "I'm not much of a talker, I'm a journalist, I write, but I do want to say, that just like when a catastrophe happens, the country always come together and support one another, no matter what race. This is that time that we need to come together". "I'm sorry, but that's all the time we could put together, I would love to have you all back for hopefully a better and much happier times where we are celebrating a difference. Oh...I would just love a hug". Kathuran hugged every one of the guest. "I am grateful for how all of this has turned out, and maybe we all can go out for a meal and discuss how we can contribute and get this ball rolling. Thanks to all of my guest, Johnny Collins, Ms. Stacy Fallings, and Mr. Jason Garrit. I am your host Kathuran McNeal. See you next time".

CHAPTER 14
(THE VIEWING OF ALL THAT IS LEFT)

"Finally", Darnell said as the sheriffs called his name while he was pacing back and forth in a holding cell awaiting his moment to see all that remained of his son. One of the Sheriffs attempted to make small talk to lighten the mood, but Darnell chose to ride in silence. When they arrived at the church, there was no one there except the pastor who met them at the door as they entered. "How are you holding up son?" Darnell know the pastor since when he was just a child, being the same pastor who had married him and Karmen while pregnant with child. "I've seen better days preach, but I would never complain". "Never have. And you know what man, this is why our God is sending blessings as we speak. Now I want to pray with you, and then I'll leave to take care of your business...yes". They walked by the casket and picture of Quincey then stopped. The pastor placed his hand on Darnell's shoulder, bowed his head and said, *"Let us pray. My God...who are always in the Heavens, and everywhere around us. Work the wheel not for, but with us Lord. This young man, a dear friend of mine...he doesn't come to you hands out requesting materials, or...monetary...no, not even the freedom that he deserves. Just for another day to do your will Lord. If I may ask uh huh...for better days ahead for the young man and his gloom, but that you bless the dead, and when you call for that day of resurrection...uh huh, that the young man we are here for today...yes, be called up front, and be forgiven, for my God is not only a loving...but a forgiving God. In your name we pray."* Yes", he said patting Darnell on the back, "Tend to your business, just give me a call on your way out". "Yes sir".

Darnel stood there for a bit, looking from the picture of his son to the casket, wondering if he may have went wrong somewhere down the line. One of the Sheriff's said, "We'll be out the doors, take your time". "Thank you", Darnell spoke in a dry voice.

"Damn. I read your letter a thousand times...you could of told me you was feeling bad. You didn't even give me a chance to be a father in a time of need, I get it son...your mind was made up, if I'm selfish, I just feel cheated is all. You had it all...right in front of you...Ahhhh...how do I piece back together your brother and sister's heart, they're broken? I'll figure it out", he spoke in between tears. *"I'm a be a grandfather, it's gonna hurt every time I look at my grandchild, and think about how much she or he looks just like you"*. He broke down when he thought about returning home next week to a house with one empty room. The pastor came flying out of his office just in time as Darnell was falling to his knees. *"I got you son"*. The pastor got down on his knee and placed his hands on Darnell's shoulders and said, *"Get it all out son, let it out...give it to God, we got you"*. The sheriff's decided to come and get Darnell and return him to the prison after two and a half hours. *"Alright son, I'll be out to see you this weekend you hear?"* *"Yes sir...thank you..."* *"No need for that, I'm here when you need me, make sure you hold your head up"*.

Other Books by the Publisher

If You 'Bout That Life!

Take Money

David L. McNair

JOHNNY COLLINS
BLOOD
Of
MY PEOPLE
Mental Bondage
BLOOD Of MY PEOPLE
JOHNNY COLLINS